W9-ABX-230

Ms. Christy Beggs
576 Butte St
Willard, OH 44890

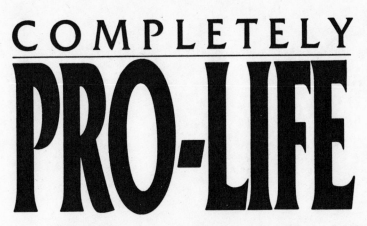

COMPLETELY PRO-LIFE

Building a Consistent Stance

Ronald J. Sider

with the staff of Evangelicals for Social Action

INTERVARSITY PRESS
DOWNERS GROVE, ILLINOIS 60515

InterVarsity Press is the book-publishing division of InterVarsity Christian Fellowship, a student movement active on campus at hundreds of universities, colleges and schools of nursing. For information about local and regional activities, write Public Relations Dept., InterVarsity Christian Fellowship, 6400 Schroeder Rd., P.O. Box 7895, Madison, WI 53707-7895.

Distributed in Canada through InterVarsity Press, 860 Denison St., Unit 3, Markham, Ontario L3R 4H1, Canada.

Cover illustration: Ed Sobieraj

ISBNs 0-8308-1706-9 (hardback)
      0-87784-496-8 (paperback)

Printed in the United States of America

Library of Congress Cataloging in Publication Data

Sider, Ronald J.
    Completely pro-life.

    Bibliography: p.
    Includes index.
    1. Social ethics. 2. Christian ethics. 3. Pro-life
movement. 4. Pacifism. 5. Peace. I. Evangelicals
for Social Action (U.S.) II. Title.
HM216.S47 1987   179'.7   87-3371
ISBN 0-8308-1706-9
ISBN 0-87784-496-8 (pbk.)

17	16	15	14	13	12	11	10	9	8	7	6	5	4	3
99	98	97	96	95	94	93	92	91	90	89				

To grandchildren yet to be,
who—please God—
may also exult in
life abundant.

Acknowledgments

Many people helped make this book possible.

Randy Elliott supplied a first draft of chapters five and seven. Norman Bendroth did the same for chapter three, and Cathy Coffin for chapter nine. Rodney Veerstra did research for the section on smoking. Numerous people in Evangelicals for Social Action, especially Executive Director Bill Kallio, Board Member Barbara Skinner and Advisory Board Member John Perkins, provided important critical reactions at various stages. Dave Zercher tracked down numerous materials. Other friends in numerous places, including Merold Westphal, Kathy Hayes, Juli Loesch, Tom McDaniel, Doug Miller, Manfred Brauch and Peter Schreck reacted critically to individual chapters. Joyce Peterman assembled the index. I thank them all without assigning them responsibility for what I was too stubborn to change.

As always, the help of my superb secretaries was invaluable. Naomi Miller's outstanding assistance on other necessary tasks that never seem to end helped provide the space for writing. And Marcia Patton again demonstrated her amazing skill of quickly and accurately deciphering the hieroglyphics of my original handwritten manuscript.

Chapter 1

Fullness of Life

The earliest Christian ethic, from Jesus to Constantine, can be described as a consistent pro-life ethic. . . . It pleaded for the poor, the weak, women, children and the unborn. This pro-life ethic discarded hate in favor of love, war in favor of peace, oppression in favor of justice, bloodshed in favor of life. The Christian's response to abortion was one important aspect of this consistent pro-life ethic.[1]
Michael J. Gorman, *Abortion and the Early Church*

"I came that they may have life, and have it abundantly." *John 10:10*

Nuclear war threatens life on a previously unimaginable scale; abortion takes life daily on a horrendous scale; public executions are fast becoming weekly events in the most advanced technological society in history; and euthanasia is now openly discussed and even advocated. . . . The case for a consistent ethic of life . . . joins the humanity of the unborn infant and the humanity of the hungry; it calls for positive legal action to prevent the killing of the unborn or the aged and positive societal action to provide shelter for the homeless and education for the illiterate.[2]
Cardinal Joseph Bernardin, *The Seamless Garment*

*E*veryone supports life. But some strange inconsistencies pop up on the way to its practical protection.

Why do many liberal and radical activists champion nuclear disarmament to protect the sanctity of human life and then defend the destruction of one-and-one-half million unborn American babies each year? Are affluent lifestyles and sexual freedom finally more important than helpless, inconvenient babies?

Why does Senator Jesse Helms, one of the most visible advocates of the pro-life (antiabortion) movement, support government subsidies for tobacco? Is the political clout of North Carolina's influential tobacco growers more important to this pro-life advocate than the fact that smoking kills 350,000 Americans a year?

Why do Marxists destroy millions and impose totalitarian governments on hundreds of millions in order to create an "ideal life for all"? Is economic justice (for the Party apparently, since the effective income differentials between Communist Party members and ordinary citizens is often greater than in capitalist societies) more important than religious and political freedom?

Why does Jerry Falwell, another pro-life champion, defend South Africa's President Botha and the Philippines' ex-President Marcos in the name of preserving freedom from Marxist revolution? Is preserving freedom (for Americans, apparently, since black South Africans and poor Filipinos certainly do not have it) more important than changing economic systems that currently condemn millions to poverty, malnutrition and death by starvation?

Why did the Southern Baptist Convention in North Carolina choose to remain silent about the devastating effects of smoking after the national body spoke out?[3] Is the moral evil of death by smoking-induced cancer less apparent to Bible-believing Christians who live in a major tobacco-growing state?

Why do many people join the crusade for nuclear disarmament and neglect poverty and starvation among the poor? Is the growing danger that a nuclear holocaust may destroy us more important to affluent Westerners than the present death by malnutrition of millions of persons?

Why do the members of the National Right to Life Committee (a major antiabortion group) score far lower on other pro-life issues like opposition to the arms race, handguns and concern for the poor than do the members of the National Abortion Rights Action League (a pro-abortion group)? Don't handguns and poverty obliterate precious human beings as surely as abortion?

What does it really mean to be pro-life? Is there a consistent pro-life stance?

The answer of course depends on one's basic values. If one endorses Marx's philosophical materialism, then sacrificing millions of people on the way to a secular utopia is not inconsistent. If one knows that the fetus is merely a physical appendage of the mother and not an independent human life, then favoring abortion and opposing nuclear war are not inconsistent. If freedom has a higher value than justice, then promoting religious and political liberty even at the expense of a decent life or even life itself for the poor is not inconsistent. It all depends on what one means by *life*.

Whether consciously or unconsciously, everyone's definition of what it means to be pro-life emerges from his or her deepest beliefs. Pluralistic societies include people with widely divergent religious and philosophical convictions. Therefore, it is inevitable that fundamentally contradictory definitions of *life* and correspondingly contradictory public-policy proposals emerge. In a pluralistic democratic society each person is free to articulate public-policy options that grow out of his or her deepest beliefs about life. Only when a majority accepts a given approach does it become law.

This book is an attempt to articulate a consistent pro-life stance on public-policy issues that flows from a biblical definition of life.

The Story of the Bible

The infinite, almighty God is the source of all life: "In his hand is the life of every living thing" (Job 12:10).[4] Out of nothing God has created all that exists. Pantheistic and monistic views which see all reality as an emanation or a part of the Divine are increasingly popular today.[5] The biblical view of creation is radically different. Every part of God's creation is very good and very special, because it all flows from the loving design of almighty God. But it is in no sense divine. It is finite, limited and dependent. Thus we must be careful when we speak of the sanctity even of human life. Persons are not sacred or holy in the sense of being divine. Christians speak of the sanctity of human life to refer to the special status humanity enjoys compared to the rest of creation.

Today, however, this special status is under attack. Some secular thinkers denounce as "speciesism" any claim that persons have a higher status than monkeys or moles.[6] The Bible, on the other hand, elevates persons to a unique status only slightly lower than the angels (Ps 8).

> Then God said, "Let us make man in our image, after our likeness; and let them have dominion over the fish of the sea, and over the birds of the air, and over the cattle, and over all the earth. . . . Be fruitful and multiply . . . and have dominion . . . over every living thing that moves upon the earth." (Gen 1:26-28)

So, according to Scripture, humanity is unique in that we are created in God's image and have dominion over the created order. But dominion is not devastation. Humanity has the special calling of gracious gardener of the good earth. We are to till, preserve and develop God's garden for our good and that of our descendants. We insult the Creator of the garden if we rape and destroy it.[7]

Nor dare we forget that from dust we have come and to dust we shall return (Gen 3:19). As finite, bodily creatures, we are interrelated with and dependent on all things.

But persons soar above the rest of creation because we alone bear the divine image. No living creature satisfied Adam apart from Eve, "bone of my bones and flesh of my flesh" (Gen 2:18-23). God gives every living thing to humanity for food (Gen 9:1-3). To be sure, God demands that we care for the rest of creation even as we use it for food (Gen 9:4). But persons are different. Only in the case of people is the shedding of blood an outrage against the Creator (9:5-7). Indeed, so precious is each human life that eventually, as the biblical story unfolds, God becomes flesh to live and suffer for the salvation of the world.

The opening chapters of Genesis sketch a glorious picture of the fullness of life intended for humanity by the Creator. A harmony of right relationships prevails everywhere—with God, with each other and with the earth. Although it is not used here, the Hebrew word *shalom* (peace) is perhaps the best word to signify this fullness of life enjoyed as Adam and Eve walk in obedient relationship to God and responsible stewardship over God's garden.

Sin, however, soon shattered this shalom. Adam and Eve rebelled against God, and so ruined their relationship with the Creator that they fled from his face in terror (Gen 3:8-10). The result was a devastating disruption of their relationships with each other and with the earth.

But God was unwilling to abandon us. Beginning with Abraham, God called out a special people to be his instrument of revelation and salvation for all. Through Moses and the prophets, the judges and the writers of wisdom, God patiently showed his chosen people how to live the abundant life.

As in the garden, God said that shalom starts with a right relationship with himself. But it also includes right relationships with our neighbor: economic justice, respect for all persons including a special concern for the poor and weak, faithful family life, fair courts and of course an end to war. Indeed, when right relationships with God and neighbor exist, humanity also experiences an abundant harmony with the earth.

Scores of texts could be cited to illustrate how the word *shalom* encompasses this fullness of life, this harmony of right relationships to which God invited the people of Israel.[8] "Great peace [*shalom*] have those who love thy law," exclaims the psalmist

(119:165). Shalom starts with love and obedience to God. On the human level, of course, it also flows from justice: "The effect of righteousness will be peace *[shalom]*" (Is 32:17; also Ps 85:10). Leviticus 26:3-6 captures this wholeness of right relationships with neighbor and the earth which flows from a proper relationship with God:

> If you walk in my statutes and observe my commandments and do them, then I will give you your rains in their season, and the land shall yield its increase, and the trees of the field shall yield their fruit. And your threshing shall last to the time of vintage, and the vintage shall last to the time for sowing; and you shall eat your bread to the full, and dwell in your land securely. And I will give peace in the land, and you shall lie down, and none shall make you afraid; and I will remove evil beasts from the land, and the sword shall not go through your land.[9]

God's covenant with Israel showed how God wanted his chosen people to relate to himself, to their neighbors and to their earth. This covenant, Malachi 2:5 indicates, was "a covenant of life and peace."[10] This fullness of life would flow from faithfulness to the covenant. But faithfulness involves a choice. Moses clarified the options at the end of Deuteronomy: life in every sense would follow if Israel obeyed God's commands, death and evil if they disobeyed. "I call heaven and earth to witness against you this day, that I have set before you life and death; . . . therefore choose life, that you and your descendants may live" (Deut 30:19).

They chose death. Worshiping idols and oppressing the poor, they defied God. So God sent first Israel and then Judah into captivity for breaking his covenant.

Still God would not give up on humanity. God's prophets looked ahead to a time when the Messiah would come to restore life and shalom (for example, Is 2:4; 9:6-7; 11:6, 9).

Jesus did precisely that. He brought a new wholeness of relationships between rich and poor, men and women—indeed, even enemies. Above all, he proclaimed and accomplished God's free forgiveness. By dying for us who rebelled against the Creator's shalom, Jesus brought peace with God (Rom 5:1). As the Spirit begins to restore our broken personalities so devastated by the death-dealing invasion of the enemy, we again experience wholeness of life. "To set the mind on the flesh is death, but to set the mind on the Spirit is life and peace" (Rom 8:6).

In Christ we receive abundant life. "I am come that they might have life, and that they might have it more abundantly" (Jn 10:10 KJV). Since Jesus and the Father are one (Jn 10:30), Jesus is the only way to fullness of life (Jn 14:6).

Increasingly since the Enlightenment of the eighteenth century, secular thinkers have promoted purely human paths to wholeness of life. If we will only offer quality education to all; if we will only modify our social environment; if we will only change the economic system; if we will only undertake this or that bit of human engineering, secular thinkers promise a new person and a new social order freed from the stupidity and selfishness of the past. The Marxist promise that utopia will follow the abolition of private property is merely one of the more naive versions of the Enlightenment's secular humanism.

Christians know this is dangerous nonsense. Certainly we can affect significant changes by improving social structures. But no amount of social engineering will create unselfish persons. Tragically, the human problem lies far deeper than mere (even very unjust) social systems. It lies in the proud, rebellious, self-centered heart of every person. A transforming relationship with the living God is the only way to heal the brokenness at the core of our being.

That is why Jesus told Nicodemus that he must be born again of the Spirit (Jn 3:1-15). It is only as we believe that God has sent his only Son to live and die for us that we experience genuine life—indeed, eternal life (Jn 3:16). As the Gospel of John says so beautifully and powerfully, eternal life begins now as we believe in Christ because "this is eternal life, that they know thee the only true God, and Jesus Christ whom thou hast sent" (17:3). As the Spirit begins to transform believers, we enjoy the first fruits of eternal life even now. Thus we enjoy an abundant life as we live in Christ, and our personalities are already being reshaped according to the pattern of his perfection.

But even the shalom of abundant Christian living pales by comparison with the glorious life of the age to come. "For to me to live is Christ, and to die is gain" was Paul's confident cry (Phil 1:21; see also Acts 20:24).

Physical human life is not the highest value. There are many things worth dying for. To say that Christians oppose the nuclear arms race because human life is exceedingly precious is not to say that life here on earth is the ultimate good. "Thy steadfast love is better than life," the psalmist exclaimed (63:3). Jesus taught that we should sacrifice eyes, limbs, possessions, indeed even life itself for the sake of the kingdom of God and the harmony of right relationships that make up the righteousness of that kingdom (Mt 18:7-9; 6:25-34; Lk 12:13-31).

Because Christians know that Jesus is the resurrection and life (Jn 11:25), Christians will sacrifice their own physical life for freedom, justice, peace and evangelism. Jesus has conquered death in all its terror. Therefore, we know that death is only a temporary transition to life even more abundant.

The biblical vision of the fullness and perfection of eternal life in the coming kingdom is finally the only adequate answer to the question: What is life really all about? What after all is genuine living? True life is eternal life in the presence of the risen Lord in a kingdom of shalom from which all the devastation of sin has been cast forth.

It is crucial to see that the biblical teaching about eternal life does not refer to some ethereal, spiritual fairyland totally unrelated to human history and the created order. Paul clearly teaches that this groaning creation will be freed of its bondage and decay and experience the glorious liberty of the children of God (Rom 8:18-25). In Colossians he describes God's cosmic plan of redemption. God intends to restore all things whether in heaven or on earth (in other words, everything in the created order) to its original wholeness and shalom (Col 1:15- 20). That is not to adopt universalism. I do not believe that all will be saved. But it is to stand with Paul in amazement at God's cosmic intention of restoring every structure of the created order.

How God will do that we do not know. The coming kingdom is certainly not a purely human construction that we weld together with slow incremental improvements. There will be fundamental disjuncture between fallen history as we know it and the shalom of heaven. Revelation 21:1-4 describes the coming kingdom as a new heaven, a new earth and a new Jerusalem. But notice on the other hand that it is a city and it is called earth. And God dwells with us, wiping away tears, banishing pain and death. Poverty, warfare, broken families and abortion will give way to an unspeakable fullness of life in the presence of the Lord of life.

There is a fundamental break between life now and the coming kingdom; but there is also significant continuity. Revelation says that the kings of the earth will bring their glory to the holy city (21:24-26). The crystalline river of life waters the tree of life whose leaves are given for the healing of the nations (22:2). Apparently God intends to transform all that is good in human culture, purify it of all sinful distortion, and make it a part of the shalom of the eternal kingdom.

Whether through personal charity, intermediate institutions or organized politics, whenever we can reshape society, however modestly, according to the norms of the coming kingdom, to that extent we erect small imperfect signs of the shalom which God will finally bring. Because we know that sin will continue to rampage through every human society until Christ returns, we abandon the naive optimism of liberalism. And because we know that the powers of the age to come are already at work, we reject the fatalistic pessimism of dispensationalism. Doing our best now, we rest content with significant yet imperfect improvements, waiting in hope for that promised fullness of right relationships between God, persons and the earth which will ultimately blaze forth in eternal splendor at the return of the King.

What a breathtaking definition of life! What a fantastic perspective on what it means to be pro-life! As those who accept this biblical vision as ultimate truth, we are called to gently care for the natural order because it comes from the hand of the Creator and is destined for inclusion in the coming kingdom. And we are to treasure and care for persons even more because the Lord of life placed men and women in charge of his garden and then became flesh to die and rise for their restoration to wholeness. Creation is so good that human life now is a joy and delight. Jesus healed many that never became his followers. So, too, Christians today seek to shape a better social order for both Christian and non-Christian. Creation is so good that merely enjoying the bounties of life, health, home and a decent social order for three-score years and ten is something the Creator desires for all.

Yet even the best life now or the most grace-filled life of the believer is nothing in comparison with the splendor of life eternal. Knowing that the destiny of persons far transcends passing political kingdoms that rise and fall, we as Christians need not tremble before tyrants or absolutize political systems. Rather, we can insist on measuring, challenging and transforming every society according to the vision of life abundant in the coming kingdom.

The Biblical Vision and the Political Process
Earlier I said the purpose of this book was to develop a consistent pro-life agenda for public policy. What does all this theology have to do with politics? Does this inspiring biblical perspective on life help in any way to make life more just and free for harassed Miskito Indians in Nicaragua or underpaid laborers on Philippine

sugar plantations? Does it tell us anything about how to rewrite the laws dealing with the unborn or the dying?

Yes. But the journey from one to the other is not simple.

To move from the Bible to concrete public-policy proposals requires at least four steps: (1) a decision to submit every political thought and action to biblical revelation rather than to ideological bias; (2) a careful analysis of the biblical material; (3) a sophisticated study of society; and (4) the formation and testing of concrete, specific proposals for public life.

The starting point is *to accept the political implications of the Christian confession that Jesus Christ is Lord.* The Bible dares to proclaim that he is now Lord of all things in heaven and on earth (Mt 28:18; Eph 1:20-22; Rev 1:5). That means that Christ and his values must be in charge of every area of the Christian's life. That includes not just our church and sexual life, but also our politics.

If Christ is head of our politics, then Jesus will set our political agenda. Typically, most Christians get their political opinions from family, friends and neighbors rather than from Jesus. Usually the particular ideological bias (whether left or right) inherited from home, school and work shapes our political thought and activity rather than Jesus. If we are serious about Jesus, however, that simply will not do. To refuse to let Jesus and his revelation set our political agenda is finally to deny that he is our Lord.

But what does it mean to let Jesus be lord of our politics? It means consciously deciding to examine every political thought and action by the standards of God's Word. It means abandoning one-issue politics and replacing it with a balanced biblical agenda concerned with all the things the Bible says God is. It means refusing to be a radical in the sixties and a neoconservative in the eighties just because the political winds have shifted. It means an unconditional resolve to vote and lobby according to the standards of Jesus' dawning kingdom rather than according to the values of the status quo.

Second, all this requires *careful biblical study.* This step in the journey from the Bible to politics requires a lot more than hastily stringing together a few proof texts. Since the entire Bible is the infallible, inspired Word of God, we must carefully examine every part of the Scripture, not just favorite passages.

The total biblical story—the long history from creation and Fall through the call of Abraham and his descendants to Christ, the church and the Second Coming—shapes every aspect of Christian ethics, including politics. And it provides the context for understanding the biblical teaching on specific issues.

If one wanted to develop a biblical perspective on a specific area such as economic justice, one would need to start with the goodness of the created order and the importance of work in Genesis; discuss the teaching on property and possessions in the Law; listen to the denunciation of economic oppression in the prophets; explore the economic sharing in Jesus' new community of disciples and the early church; and finally, wonder at the eschatological vision of the time when Christ returns to wipe away the tears of the oppressed and hungry.

Careful biblical exegesis would be necessary at every point. So would attention to hermeneutical assumptions, including one's view of the relationship between the Old and New Testaments. Carefully, systematically, one would put together a comprehensive summary or paradigm[11] of biblical teaching on a given issue as that develops and is amplified in all the different strands of biblical thought.

As one developed comprehensive summaries or paradigms on all the different topics and issues, one would come to see more clearly the interrelationship of biblical themes and the balance of biblical concerns. As one discovered that the Bible says a great deal about both personal and social sin, both the family and justice for the poor, both peace and the value of human life, one would resolve to reject all political agendas focused narrowly on only one or two issues.

This second step of careful biblical study really involves several substeps: attention to the total biblical story; the development of comprehensive summaries or paradigms on particular topics like the family or economic justice (always paying attention to careful exegesis and proper principles of biblical interpretation); and the articulation of a balanced biblical agenda of concerns.

But even then the work is only half done. Old Testament laws required the execution of homosexuals and rebellious children, the return of the land to the original owners every fifty years and the forgiveness of loans every seven years. I do not believe God wants American, German or Indian governments today to legislate these specific provisions.[12] Rather, God wants us to apply the biblical material as one applies a paradigm. To some degree, because the modern world differs enormously from rural Palestine, the specific provisions will differ. But the principles and norms remain the same. It is only as we develop concrete public-policy proposals that clearly reflect biblical principles about the nature of the family, work and justice that we can say that God's revelation shapes our political proposals.

The fact that contemporary society is vastly different from biblical times underlines the importance of step three: we must undertake a *sophisticated study of society*. The most careful socioeconomic-political analysis is essential. This includes everything from getting one's facts straight about the actual number of unemployed or homeless persons to developing broad historical generalizations based on a careful study of history. An example of the latter would be a judgment about the overall impact of Western colonialism, Marxist revolutions or multinational corporations. Such historical generalizations relate directly to one's political solutions for, say, contemporary poverty in the Third World. Such sweeping historical judgments are complex and difficult. But they are an unavoidable element of relating the biblical paradigms to contemporary society.

Finally, in the fourth step, we need to *propose and test very specific proposals for public policy*. It is not good enough to say that the Bible demands justice for the poor. Christians need to say concretely what that biblical concern means for reshaping current policy on welfare or economic foreign aid. To do that requires an application of the biblical paradigms to the complexities of modern society. Normally that requires an organization or think tank that includes many specialists from several disciplines, including biblical studies, ethics and the social sciences.

Good theoretical proposals, however, are not enough. They need careful testing. Sometimes seemingly good ideas have unfortunate, unforeseen side effects. Therefore, careful experimentation with new public proposals is essential.

You may feel that the process just outlined is overwhelmingly complex and difficult. Surely I am not suggesting that the average layperson go through this entire process before entering the polling booth. Of course not. That would be impossible. We all need the support and insight of other sisters and brothers who have skills and experiences we lack. The sophisticated analysis described above can be done in our colleges, seminaries, think tanks and public-policy organizations like Bread for the World, the Association for Public Justice and Evangelicals for Social Action.

This book, in fact, is one very modest attempt to implement the methodology just outlined. Unfortunately, the task is so large and my expertise (even when assisted by the staff of Evangelicals for Social Action) is so limited that the method is only very imperfectly followed. If, however, this book succeeds in suggesting a method and a direction for others to develop, that will be enough.

What Should We Legislate?

Virtually all Western nations are pluralistic secular societies. Many different religions are present. So too are fundamentally contradictory visions about the nature of a good society.

When then should Christians who are committed to a biblically balanced pro-life agenda, try to legislate? If Christ is Lord and biblical revelation is true, should they try to impose Christian faith and ethics on everyone by legislation?

Deciding what to legislate and what to leave to individual choice is a crucial, complex problem. Without pretending to solve this difficult issue here, I will suggest three basic principles that help us toward an answer:

First, *the church should first model in its own life what it calls on the government to legislate.* It is a farce for the church to ask Washington to legislate what Christians refuse to live. The first application of biblical truth is to those who confess Christ. The church ought to be far ahead of the rest of society in implementing biblical norms. Unlike the rest of society, Christians experience the liberating power of divine forgiveness, the regenerating and sanctifying presence of the Holy Spirit, the encouragement of other believers and the strength that comes from knowing revealed truth. For all these reasons, the church should be able to practice justice, freedom and shalom far more fully than unbelievers. That does not mean that the church must be perfect before Christians enter the political arena. But it does mean that Christians lack credibility and clout unless their local congregations are already starting to believe and model what they call on government to legislate.

Second, *Christians should not use the state to impose religious beliefs on others.* The separation of church and state is not merely a pragmatic necessity in a pluralistic society. Religious faith by its very nature is a free response to God. It cannot be coerced. Throughout biblical history we see a sovereign God constantly inviting persons into free dialog. God invites obedience but is astonishingly patient with those who decline the invitation. If the history of Israel tells us anything, it discloses how much space God gives people to reject his will and still continue to enjoy the created gifts of food, health and life. Jesus' parable of the wheat and tares (Mt 13:24-30) makes it clear that God chooses to allow believers and nonbelievers to live and enjoy the world together until the end of history. Since God intends history to be the place where people have the freedom to respond or not respond to him, the state should not promote or hinder religious belief.

Sometimes, however, the separation of church and state is confused with the separation of public life from ethical values grounded in religious faith. To make the charge that Jerry Falwell's political activity violates the separation of church and state, as columnists in the *New York Times* have, is absurd. He is only doing what the National Council of Churches and Jewish organizations have done for decades. His political proposals may be unwise or insufficiently biblical, but his proposing them hardly violates the separation of church and state.

Every major political decision, every debated public-policy proposal, finally depends on basic value judgments. These in turn are rooted in religious belief. Our political views, not just on abortion and the nuclear arms race, but on foreign policy toward Central America and the shape of the tax structure as well, are all in part dependent on basic ethical commitments, whether they are conscious or unconscious. It would be as impossible as it would be immoral to try to separate public life from ethical values grounded in religious belief.

Every citizen is free to propose to the body politic a vision and a set of concrete public-policy proposals for society that come from his or her most basic religious beliefs. In a pluralistic democratic society those proposals can become law only if a majority agree. If biblical revelation represents God's truth about the world and persons (as Christians believe), then public-policy proposals made by Christians about economic justice or the family will with some frequency (although not always) make sense and appeal to many citizens, including some who do not share those religious foundations.

One other brief comment on the separation of church and state is especially important. Probably the best protection against political totalitarianism is the recognition that the state is not the ultimate source of value and law. If people in a society believe strongly that there exists a higher law grounded in God the Creator to which current legislation ought to conform and which citizens ought to obey even if that means civil disobedience, totalitarianism will be held in check.

But how can a secular state which is neutral toward religious conviction recognize the fact that governmental activity and law are finally accountable to God? In the United States we have done things like approving state-sponsored prayer in public schools. But that is both inconsistent with the separation of church and state and a violation of the religious person's understanding of true worship as a free response to God. I believe that the responsibility for articulating this important protection against totalitarianism must be carried not by the state, but by religious bodies and religious individuals in politics. Large numbers of devout politicians, inculcated by their churches and synagogues with a deep awareness that they are finally accountable to God, will be a far better way to preserve the societal understanding that the state is not ultimate than will lobbying for state-sponsored prayer in schools. There is no reason why presidents, cabinet members and congressional leaders cannot frequently express in public their own personal conviction that no government is absolute and that all actions including those of the highest officials are subject to a higher law. Frequent personal, albeit public acknowledgment of this conviction in no way violates the separation of church and state. Yet it does promote general acceptance of this crucial concept.

Third, *Christians should not use the state to make it illegal to violate biblical ethical norms except where such violations harm the rights of others.* (The churches, of course, should have their own internal mechanisms for dealing with sins such as lying, adultery and racist attitudes.) This principle follows from the second. Persons should be free to harm themselves and consenting associates (with, for instance, adultery or excessive use of alcohol) without breaking civil laws as long as they do not harm others or infringe on their rights. Therefore, laws against racial prejudice in the sale or rental of housing are appropriate. Laws making adultery a civil offense, on the other hand, would be a mistake.

Obviously this general principle does not solve all problems. Alcoholic mothers or fathers and adulterous spouses harm their families as well as themselves. That injury, however, extends to a relatively small number of people who have a special commitment to each other. Racial discrimination in housing, on the other hand, affects a whole class of people without any consent on their part. The very nature of the family entails an implied consent that all members share both the positive and negative aspects of family life. This mutual commitment, and the family's existence as an intermediate association independent of the state, means that the state should not intervene in the family. (There are exceptions, of course: in extreme situations such as serious physical abuse of spouse or children, or denial of medical treatment necessary for survival.) Citizens should be free to break accepted (or biblical) ethical norms without legal penalty except where such infractions violate the rights of others.

Toward a Balanced Biblical Agenda
Earlier we saw that if Christians in politics want to make any claim that Christ is Lord of their political life, then they must adopt a political agenda that reflects the balance of concerns suggested by biblical revelation. That perhaps is the best test of whether one's political agenda is shaped by ideological bias or Christian faith.

At the beginning of this chapter we saw some strikingly inconsistent examples where people affirmed one part of a biblical pro-life agenda and ignored others. Others abound. In an interview in *Christianity Today,* Jerry Falwell explicitly said that Moral Majority does not deal with the issue of justice for the poor: "We could never bring the issue of the poor into Moral Majority. . . . We just have to stay away from helping the poor."[13] That simply will not do if Jerry Falwell wants a biblical pro-life agenda. According to God's Word, human life matters after birth as well as before.

One sees the same imbalance in Falwell's *Newsweek* column: "Freedom is the ultimate moral issue."[14] Falwell is undoubtedly correct that biblical principles summon Christians to a ringing endorsement of freedom—religious freedom, political freedom, due process of law and a pluralistic democratic process. I believe deeply that biblical values point toward the freedom of democracy rather than the slavery of totalitarianism. Positively, the Bible teaches that each person is called by God to be a coworker in the shaping of history. Democracy, when it really works, enables that to happen. Negatively, biblical faith teaches that because of sin, power tends to corrupt and absolute power tends to corrupt absolutely. Therefore, it is essential that power be decentralized in human society if we are to have either justice or freedom.

Falwell is right in treasuring freedom. But he is unbiblical when he makes freedom the overriding moral issue. The Bible says at least as much about justice. If the Bible sets the agenda, then we will emphasize justice as much as freedom. Today, "liberals" are inclined to stress justice more than freedom. Conservatives often value freedom more than justice. One crucial test of whether Christian political activity is free of ideological bias from both left and right will be whether it emphasizes both freedom and justice in equal measure.

A hasty survey of the current religious scene in the United States might lead one to despair of a political consensus for a consistent pro-life agenda. But that would be a superficial judgment. Increasingly today, especially in the churches, there is a growing movement of folk who care about justice and freedom, the sanctity of unborn life and the lives of the poor, the family and the environment, an end to murder on the highways, and the nuclear arms race.

One sees signs of a potential new coalition in an organization like Pro Lifers for Survival, an ecumenical antiabortion group strongly opposed to the nuclear arms race. One sees it when Nat Hentoff, a New York liberal activist, changes his mind on abortion and pleads with secular liberal activists to reject abortion.[15] One sees it when *Sojourners* magazine, long known for its condemnation of injustice and militarism, comes out against abortion.[16] One sees it when a *Sojourners*-sponsored Peace Pentecost (1985) protests not only U.S. policy in Central America and the ongoing arms race, but also abortion on demand and the Soviet invasion of Afghanistan.[17] One sees it when Evangelicals for Social Action defines its program as a consistent pro-life agenda concerned to protect the family and the environment, oppose abortion and the nuclear arms race, and seek both justice and liberty.[18] One sees it when mainline, "pro-choice" denominations re-examine their stand on abortion. One sees it when a broad coalition of Protestants and Catholics form JustLife, a new political action committee that supports candidates who oppose abortion and the nuclear arms race and support economic justice.[19] One sees it when Lutheran bishop Lowell O. Erdahl publishes a new book called *Pro-Life/Pro-Peace*.[20]

Most publicly and visibly, one sees it when the U.S. Catholic bishops issue a ringing call for nuclear disarmament and link it to their long opposition to abortion.[21] Cardinal Joseph Bernardin of Chicago headed the committee that drafted this historic document adopted in May 1983. It is significant that that fall the bishops elected him chairman of their pro-life committee (their antiabortion structure) and that he proceeded to give widely publicized speeches on "The Seamless Garment." In those speeches he insisted that we must apply everywhere the principle that "the directly intended taking of innocent human life is immoral."

The principle . . . cannot be successfully sustained on one account and simultaneously eroded in a similar situation. . . . Asking . . . questions along the spectrum of life from womb to tomb creates the need for a consistent ethic of life. For the spectrum of life cuts across the issue of genetics, abortion, capital punishment, modern warfare and the case of the terminally ill. . . .

Success on any one of the issues threatening life requires a concern for the broader attitude in society about respect for human life.[22]

This book will achieve its purpose if it makes a contribution to this developing coalition of people committed to a consistent pro-life agenda.

Part 1

ABORTION

Chapter 2

Biblical Faith
and the Unborn

We can no longer base our ethics on the idea that human beings are a special
form of creation, singled out from all other animals, and alone possessing an
immortal soul.[1]
Peter Singer

So God created man in his own image, in the image of God he created him;
male and female he created them. **Genesis 1:27**

Two contradictory views about persons struggle for domi-
nance today. For some contemporaries, people are merely
complex animals, an accidental product of blind materialistic processes. Self-fulfillment and usefulness to society determine
dignity and value. For others, every person is the conscious creation of a loving God and reflects the very image of the Creator
of the galaxies. Human dignity, value and worth come not primarily from the state, society or self-actualization but from God as a
sheer gift.

The struggle to maintain the historic Christian belief in the
inestimable value of every person rages on many fronts—genetic
engineering, euthanasia, infanticide, abortion. Here, I focus on
abortion.

Protecting the Sanctity of Human Life

For many American Protestants awareness of the abortion issue began in 1973 with the historic decision of the U.S. Supreme Court, Roe vs. Wade. This ruling swept aside laws in fifty states limiting the availability of abortions. The court decreed that the state had no "compelling interest" in protecting the unborn child until it was "viable" or "capable of meaningful human life"—in other words, for the first six months or "usually" (according to the court's reckoning) for the first seven months of pregnancy.

Even after "viability," the ruling went, the fetus is not a human being "in the whole sense" and the Fourteenth Amendment's guarantee that life shall not be taken without due process does not apply. A state may not prohibit abortion even at this late stage if the health of the mother is at risk. And the court defined *health* very broadly: health is a medical judgment "exercised in the light of all factors—physical, emotional, familial, and the woman's age—relevant to the well-being of the patient." Even a nine-month-old fetus can be sacrificed for the "emotional" health of the mother.[2]

As a result of this ruling, abortion on demand became legal. Each year since then, about 1.5 million abortions have occurred in the United States. How are Christians to respond? First, it is imperative that those of us who feel abortion is a travesty and an affront to God still demonstrate genuine empathy for the dilemmas and anguish of the millions of women who have sought abortions. For any Christian discussion of the topic, we must understand the tormented options facing the fifteen-year-old whose mistaken choices have produced an unwanted pregnancy that seems to threaten her entire future. Anyone who has sympathetically observed the burdens placed on a family struggling for decades to care for a seriously handicapped child understands how tempting abortion may seem to a couple informed that the fetus may be severely handicapped. How does one tell the victim of rape or incest that she must sacrifice herself for nine long months to nurture the unwanted seed of a vicious aggressor?

Honest struggle with the strength of pro-abortion arguments is also essential for those of us who wish to persuade those who adhere to these arguments. Women have experienced widespread discrimination and oppression for centuries. Their demand, however strident and overstated it may sometimes be, for the freedom to choose whether or not to give birth to a child which will probably impact her life more than that of the (frequently irresponsible) father is understandable. There is a global population problem today. Those overcrowded countries (Japan and China, for example) that have been most successful in quickly slowing their population explosions have adopted abortion as one measure. Whether in America's inner cities or in the slums of Latin America, some poor women already burdened with poverty and several children do seek abortions regardless of what the law or the church says. Many ask, Should we add to their trauma with laws that guarantee that their abortionists will be unqualified hacks in dirty back rooms rather than trained physicians in sanitary settings?

What also seems confusing to many is to notice that religious people, including evangelical Christians, cannot agree on whether the fetus is a fully human being. According to Kenneth Kantzer, former editor of *Christianity Today*, "No Biblical passage speaks of man or fully human life before birth or condemns abortion as murder."[3] A major consultation of evangelicals—including Harold Lindsell, Carl Henry and Harold J. Ockenga—in 1968 issued an Affirmation that said: "As to whether or not the performance of an individual abortion is always sinful, we are not agreed, but about the necessity and permissibility for it under certain circumstances, we are in accord."[4] The Affirmation included "individual health, family welfare, and social responsibility" among values that might warrant an induced abortion.[5] Today many of those at this conference would put the matter differently. But the conference certainly demonstrates the point that there has been major disagreement among evangelical Protestants.[6] Carl Henry still considers abortion morally justified in the case of rape, incest and "extreme deformity" of the fetus.[7]

On the other hand, no one except extreme male chauvinists doubt that the pregnant mother is truly a person with full human rights. In light of the uncertainty and disagreement about the status of the fetus as well as the strength of the arguments for abortion, one can understand why many compassionate people of good will consider abortion morally acceptable.

A decade ago, I found these arguments conclusive. But troubling doubts and disturbing questions have caused me to change my thinking: Does not the swift, easy transition from abortion to experimentation on fetuses to inappropriately withholding treatment to promotion of euthanasia suggest a dangerous assault on the sacredness of human life? Does not the level of trauma experienced after abortions suggest greater caution? Is the witness of church history irrelevant? And do not both individuals and society frequently support abortion for selfish, irresponsible reasons?

A Slippery Slope?

Is it not likely that permitting abortions also encourages experimenting on fetuses and growing acceptance of policies that withhold treatment from deformed children? Using federal money, a medical school in Los Angeles has conducted experiments on unborn fetuses scheduled for abortion.[8] Others have experimented on live fetuses *after* abortion, placing them in tanks of saline solution.[9] In Europe, according to a report by a research committee of the European Parliament, living aborted fetuses are dissected for research by the cosmetics industry to improve beauty aids.[10]

In a powerful article in the January 1985 issue of the *Atlantic Monthly*, civil libertarian Nat Hentoff reported on examples of what he called "infanticide." Even though many of them can live successful lives, "it is common in the United States to withhold routine surgery and medical care from infants with Down's syndrome [or spina bifida] for the explicit purpose of hastening death."[11] In the October 25, 1973, issue of *The New England Journal of Medicine*, two Yale doctors reported on forty-three babies who died because the doctors withheld treatment. Since these handicapped babies would have placed long-term emotional and financial stress on the parents, parents and doctors chose not to provide available treatment. So they died.[12] Deciding not to undertake extraordinary measures in cases where there is no hope of recovery is one thing. Failing to perform operations that would enable babies to live and enjoy life in spite of severe handicaps is quite another. It is infanticide. Fortunately, President Reagan moved to protect handicapped infants in 1983. And the 1984 amendments to the Child Abuse Prevention and Treatment Act require that all states receiving federal grants for child abuse make certain that handicapped infants receive available treatment.

Widespread encouragement of euthanasia may not be far away.[13] Some folk call attention to the fact that eleven per cent of all Medicare funds support people in the last forty days of their lives and twenty-five per cent go to elderly folk in the last year of their life.[14] On March 27, 1984, Governor Richard Lamm of Colorado suggested in a public speech that terminally ill elderly persons have "a duty to die and get out of the way."[15]

With growing frequency prominent people defend these developments with statements explicitly rejecting the historic Judeo-Christian respect for human life. Nobel prize winner Francis Crick has said: "No newborn infant should be declared human until it has passed certain tests regarding its genetic endowment and . . . if it fails these tests, it forfeits the right to live."[16] *Newsweek* reported in 1985 that Dr. Virginia Abernathy of Vanderbilt's School of Medicine claims that an individual becomes a person only when he or she becomes a "responsible moral agent—around age three or four in Abernathy's judgment."[17]

To be sure, slippery-slope arguments are treacherous. We dare not reject something good merely because it might theoretically encourage or lead to some danger or abuse. But in light of current practice and far more radical proposals, is it neurotic and irresponsible to ask with civil libertarian Nat Hentoff: "If fetuses have no rights, handicapped infants have no rights, can the aged and infirm be far behind?"[18]

Emotional Cost

Wrenching personal stories and scholarly studies of abortion's psychological costs also urge caution. A study reported in the *Scientific American* found that ninety-two per cent of mothers who had abortions on medical grounds later suffered depression.[19] Eighty-two per cent of the fathers also experienced depression.[20] In a stream of articles in pro-choice magazines like *Glamour, Mademoiselle* and *Redbook,* women have shared their anguish and guilt.[21]

> I am angry at Billie Jean King and Gloria Steinem and every woman who ever had an abortion and didn't tell me about this kind of pain. There is a conspiracy among the sisterhood not to tell each other about guilt and self-hatred and terror. Having an abortion is not like having a wart removed or your nails done or your hair cut, and anyone who tells you it is is a liar or worse. To decide to have an abortion is to make a life-and-death decision. A part of me is dying too.[22]

In Japan, Buddhist temples attempt to alleviate the pain of grieving mothers. At a cost of $340 to $640 each, they have erected over 10,000 small statues for the aborted. For a fee of $40 to $120, temple priests also contract to pray for the aborted. "We will give the best possible care to the soul of your unborn child." In the first seven years of the program, women paid the temple to pray for 120,000 aborted children.[23]

In a recent article in *Child Psychiatry and Human Development,* Dr. Philip Ney cited a number of studies showing that living children whose mothers had also had abortions suffer trauma. They fear that parental love is conditional. "The haunted child survives to live in distrust of what may be in store for him."[24] Dr. Ney also found that child abuse is more frequent among mothers who have previously had an abortion.[25] Stanley Hauerwas's poignant question is surely relevant: "How do we tell our children what we are doing and still make them glad that they are our children?"[26]

Christian History

Christian witness over two millennia presents a third reason for caution. In an important book published by Harvard University Press, John T. Noonan concludes from his survey of church history that fetal life has enjoyed "an almost absolute value in Christian history."[27] Unfortunately, as feminists point out, this historical rejection of abortion was often mixed with an extremely negative attitude toward sex itself. Theologians like St. Augustine attacked both abortion and contraception, insisting that unless the purpose of sexual activity was procreation, it was sinful.[28]

The earliest Christian condemnation of abortion, however, arose for a different reason. In his excellent overview of the early church's unanimous rejection of abortion, *Abortion and the Early Church*, Michael Gorman shows that the reason for this stand was a concern for the fetus. It is true that by the end of the second century, Christians generally believed that contraception was wrong because they thought procreation was the sole purpose of sex. Gorman, however, shows that the church's antiabortion stand came earlier than this position on contraception. It is significant that the earliest Christian opposition to abortion arose in Jewish Christian churches with a strong Jewish heritage which did not oppose contraception. Furthermore, they discussed the two issues—contraception and abortion—in different contexts. Early Christian writers usually condemned abortion in sections dealing with violence, murder and infanticide. Contraception, on the other hand, they usually discussed in their treatment of marriage. "Early Christian opposition to abortion, then, did not arise because abortion was seen as a means of interrupting the natural course of sexual relations but because it was viewed as murder."[29] From the early Christian writers on, most Christians over the centuries have condemned abortion.[30] One cannot lightly reject twenty centuries of Christian conviction.

Selfish Motivations

Finally, the selfish, even trivial motivations that lead to some (not all) abortions strengthen growing doubts. Nat Hentoff says he knows women who have chosen to abort because they disliked their fetus's gender![31] The study of sociologist Kristin Luker suggests that economic considerations play a significant role. The typical pro-life activist is a married woman who has three or more children. She does not work outside the home and the family income is $30,000. The typical pro-choice activist, on the other hand, is a married woman with two children. She works outside the home and the family income is over $50,000.[32] Is abortion justified if a major motivation is the desire to continue enjoying the affluence made possible by two incomes in the family?

In the larger society, too, economic concerns are important. Quietly it is hinted that it is cheaper for society to permit poor women to abort than to expand the welfare rolls. Materials on abortion produced by Planned Parenthood and similar organizations frequently present this argument.[33] Similarly, aborting potentially handicapped fetuses is more convenient than increasing societal funding for services for the handicapped. What some only whisper, an editorial in *The New Republic* was candid enough to say clearly. This editorial admits that abortion is no different from euthanasia, but insists that the social cost of caring for all the aborted fetuses is too high.[34] To what extent is the issue really affluence versus respect for the sanctity of human life?

One can hardly avoid remembering the Nazi defense of genocide, enunciated in 1935 by Arthur Gueth, director of public health in Nazi Germany:

The ill-conceived "love of thy neighbor" has to disappear, es-

pecially in relation to inferior or asocial creatures. It is the supreme duty of a national state to grant life and livelihood only to the healthy and hereditarily sound portion of the people to secure the maintenance of a hereditarily sound and racially pure folk for all eternity. The life of an individual has meaning only in the light of that ultimate aim, that is in the light of his meaning to his family and to his national state.[35]
Is concern for one's affluent lifestyle any more defendable than purity of the race? Is abortion justified to preserve one's affluence?

Male sexual irresponsibility is also a significant factor in abortions. Linda Bird Francke has shown that the most significant factor in the decision to abort is the relationship with the male partner.[36] According to demographer Judith Blake, the strongest support for legal abortion comes from affluent white men. Feminist theologian Beverly Harrison is probably correct in concluding that this male preference is because many men "value women's greater sexual availability when abortion is legal."[37] But do women make progress by demanding the "freedom" to imitate this selfish male irresponsibility and frivolous approach to sexuality? This is precisely what Harrison does when she argues that apart from elective abortion, women have no moral choice with regard to pregnancy.[38] Vernie Dale rightly debunks the underlying assumption that a woman has no "control over her own body until *after* a male partner is finished with it."[39] As Dale insists, female sexual irresponsibility is also a problem. Abstention from intercourse outside marriage is always a possibility—albeit one that Harrison never advocates! Might it not be better to challenge men to fidelity rather than to facilitate their flight from responsibility?

Even more disturbing is the suggestion of Beverly Harrison that "the well-being of a woman and the value of her life plan" matter more than the life of the unborn regardless of the status of the unborn.[40] Harrison postpones her discussion of whether the fetus is truly human until near the end of her book. She does that precisely because she thinks that question—however one answers it!—is less important than the "well-being" and "life plan" of the mother. But what if the fetus is truly a person? Does a woman's "life plan" justify murder?

At its core, as Ginny Earnest Soley points out in a superb article in *Sojourners,* the problem is a secular individualism that makes the self-interest of the individual the highest value.[41] By their sexual irresponsibility and failure to share fairly in the burdens of child care and parenting, many men have placed their individual selfish concerns above the rights of children, women and the larger community. Now in the name of the same destructive, individualistic selfishness, secular feminists demand abortion as part of their right to "reproductive freedom," appealing to that very individualism which has long led many men to trample on the needs of children and the larger community. The solution surely is for both men and women to abandon secular individualism and refuse to place self above others.

Biblical Teaching
The dignity and worth of every human being flows from divine decree, not human decision.[42] Our essential humanity does not come from government, social interaction or self-actualization. It comes from the Creator of the galaxies who selected human beings alone out of all the created order to bear the divine image (Gen 1:28). God prohibits murder. It is precisely because the neighbor bears this unique divine stamp that murder is wrong (Gen 9:6). So precious, indeed, is every person that the Sovereign of history suffered the hell of Roman crucifixion so that whoever believes may live forever in the presence of the living God.

Christians therefore ought to reject every notion that makes human dignity and value depend on some humanly defined quality of life, some individually chosen level of self-fulfillment, or some societally determined level of social usefulness. No matter how poor and defenseless, old and weak, crippled and deformed, young and helpless, human beings enjoy God-given worth and dignity that sets them apart from the rest of creation.

This crucial foundation, however, does not settle the question of abortion. Abortion is wrong only if we ought to act on the assumption that the fetus is truly human. Is that the case?

The Scriptures nowhere explicitly teach that the fetus is a person. At the same time, there are signs which point in that direction. The Bible very often uses words for the fetus that are normally applied to persons already born (Gen 25:22; 38:27-30; Job 1:21; 3:3, 11-19; 10:18-19; 31:15; Is 44:2, 24; 49:5; Jer 20:14-18; Hos 12:3). Thus Luke calls Elizabeth's unborn child a "baby" *(brephos)* (Lk 1:41, 44).

Biblical passages frequently assume significant personal continuity between the unborn and the child after birth (for instance, Jer 1:5; Ps 51:5). Psalm 139:13-16 is perhaps the most striking example:

For thou didst form my inward parts,
 thou didst knit me together in my mother's womb.
I praise thee, for thou art fearful and wonderful.
 Wonderful are thy works!
Thou knowest me right well;
 my frame was not hidden from thee,
when I was being made in secret,
 intricately wrought in the depths of the earth.
Thy eyes beheld my unformed substance;
 in thy book were written, every one of them,
the days that were formed for me,
 when as yet there was none of them.

The personal pronouns ("Thou didst knit *me* together in *my* mother's womb") indicate that the psalmist assumed that there was a direct link between himself as an adult and the tiny being that God had lovingly watched over in his mother's womb.

We need to be careful, however, not to press the biblical material beyond what it clearly says. Although strongly opposed to abortion, the careful study by the Orthodox Presbyterian Church

(OPC) wisely insists that "there is _no way to demonstrate_, either from Scripture or from science or from some combination of the two, that the unborn child _is_ a human person from the point of conception."[43] This study points out that Jeremiah 1:5 uses a personal pronoun for Jeremiah even before conception: "Before I formed you in the womb, I knew you." No one would want to argue that Jeremiah was a person even before his conception![44] Furthermore, as my colleague Professor Tom McDaniel has pointed out to me, the ancient Near East tended to see all reality as personal. Therefore one dare not place too much weight on the personal pronouns here. The OPC document goes on to reject arguments adduced to prove that the fetus is a person based on John the Baptist's leaping in the womb, the Incarnation and Psalm 51:5.[45] We dare not claim that the Bible explicitly teaches that the fetus from conception is a person.

Does the Bible ever suggest the opposite? Does the Bible provide any hint that the unborn child is less than a human being? Some have found this suggestion in Exodus 21:22-24:

> When men strive together, and hurt a woman with child, so that there is a miscarriage, and yet no harm follows, the one who hurt her shall be fined, according as the woman's husband shall lay upon him; and he shall pay as the judges determine. If any harm follows, then you shall give life for life, eye for eye, tooth for tooth, hand for hand, foot for foot, burn for burn, wound for wound, stripe for stripe.

This RSV translation (and a majority of commentators) understands this difficult text to mean that if the fetus is killed and a miscarriage follows, the penalty is a mere fine. On the other hand, if the mother is hurt or killed, then the penalty is an eye for eye or a life for a life. Many consequently conclude that the fetus has less value than the mother. Therefore, the fetus is not yet a person and abortion is permissible.[46]

Such an inference does not follow, however, even if one accepts the RSV translation. The text talks only about accidental killing.

Furthermore, even accidental killing of the unborn is punished. Surely intentional destruction of the unborn would merit more severe punishment. "How can we defend the *intentional* destruction of the unborn on the basis of a passage which condemns even its *accidental* destruction?[47]

Furthermore, the absence of the death penalty for the accidental killing of the fetus does not mean the fetus is not seen as a person. The Mosaic Law did not normally prescribe a mandatory death penalty for accidental killing (Ex 21:13-14, 20-21).

Substantial considerations, furthermore, suggest that the RSV translation may be wrong. There is no linguistic basis for arguing that Exodus 21:22 refers to a miscarriage. The literal meaning of the Hebrew is simply, "Her children came out." The noun in the singular is *yeled*, which is the normal word for "child." The verb *(yatza')* means "to go out." This verb is very often employed to refer to the ordinary birth of a normal child and is not used elsewhere in the Bible to refer to a miscarriage.[48]

The translation in the New International Version is probably better:

> If men who are fighting hit a pregnant woman and she gives birth prematurely but there is no serious injury, the offender must be fined whatever the woman's husband demands and the court allows. But if there is serious injury, you are to take life for life, eye for eye, tooth for tooth, hand for hand, foot for foot. (Ex 21:22-24)

In the first case the physical contact results in a premature birth, but baby and mother live. The fine is for the trauma of the dangerous, premature birth.[49] In the second case, if either the baby or the mother suffers harm, an equivalent penalty is exacted.

Neither this nor the previous reading of Exodus 21:22-24 suggests that the fetus is less than a person. In fact, nowhere in the Bible is there any hint that the unborn child is less than a human person from the moment of conception.

One other consideration is important. We need to ask about the

relevance of the scientific fact that from the moment of conception a genetically distinct human being exists.[50] Nowhere has this
"fact" been put more bluntly than in a pro-abortion editorial in
California Medicine, the official journal of the California Medical
Association:

> Since the old ethic [the traditional Christian viewpoint] has not
> been fully displaced, it has been necessary to separate the idea
> of abortion from the idea of killing, which continues to be
> socially abhorrent. The result has been a curious avoidance of
> the scientific fact, which everyone really knows, that human life
> begins at conception and is continuous whether intra- or extra-
> uterine until death. The very considerable semantic gymnastics
> which are required to rationalize abortion as anything but tak-
> ing human life would be ludicrous if they were not often put
> forth under socially impeccable auspices.[51]

Mere biological continuity by itself, of course, tells us nothing
about whether the *imago dei* is truly present. But it does become
relevant and significant when one remembers the scriptural
understanding of the person as a body-soul unity. The prestigious
German scholar Gerhard von Rad points out that the biblical
teaching that persons possess the image *(tselem)* and likeness *(de-
muth)* of God "refers to the whole man and do[es] not relate solely
to his spiritual and intellectual being."[52] Oliver O'Donovan, now
Regius Professor at Oxford, rightly objects to the way this body-
soul unity is ignored when the question of abortion arises: "In a
period when the most orthodox of current orthodoxies in theo-
logical anthropology has been that the Bible teaches 'body-soul
unity,' it is ironical that Christians should have allowed their view
of the fetal soul to drift upon a sea of speculation without seeking
anchorage in any account of the fetal body."[53]

The Bible teaches that each person is a body-soul unity. Science
tells us that from conception there exists a genetically distinct
human being with a continuous biological development. Surely
the most responsible conclusion is that we ought to act on the

assumption that from conception the developing fetus is truly a human being made in the image of the Creator.

To be sure, there is no explicit biblical teaching that unambiguously asserts such a view. But not a word in the Scriptures suggests the contrary. Much in the Bible tends to point in this direction. If we remain agnostic, uncertain when the developing fetus becomes truly human, we have no choice but to adopt this working assumption. If there is any serious possibility that we are dealing with human beings, we must reject abortion. To do otherwise would be like shooting blindly into a darkened theater with the justification that we cannot know whether we will hit empty seats or murder innocent people.[54]

Christians then should conclude that from the moment of conception we must act on the assumption that we are dealing with persons created in God's image. Choosing to end the life of innocent persons is wrong. It is murder. Abortion, therefore, is wrong except when the physical life of the mother is threatened (for instance, tubal pregnancy or cancer of the uterus).

But that conclusion involves some wrenching, problematic cases. What about the population explosion or the mental health of the mother? Or the much harder cases of serious deformity, rape and incest?

Hard Cases
Although sometimes exaggerated, overpopulation is a genuine problem today. It is essential that countries like Mexico and India slow down their population explosions. Abortion has played a significant role in the reduced growth rates already achieved in places like China and Japan.

But murder is not an acceptable way to solve population problems. If abortion is acceptable as a policy for population control, so is killing young children. Surely Paul Ramsey is correct that any argument for abortion that also justifies infanticide is clearly wrong.[55] Abortion is an unacceptable form of birth control.[56] Increased research on nonabortive birth-control techniques is therefore essential.

Would an apparent danger to the mental life of the mother justify abortion? As a matter of fact, the scientific evidence seems to suggest that abortion seldom if ever improves the mental health of the mother.[57]

But if it did, would it be morally justified? Not if the unborn is treated as truly human. We would not endorse killing a one-year-old child or an elderly parent merely because caring for either created severe emotional strain or even the threat of suicide.

Let us imagine a daughter caring for a difficult, but not senile, mother in an area where neither Social Services nor neighbors were available to help her bear the load. The doctor judges that the daughter is heading for a major, and permanent, breakdown, and sees no way of avoiding it short of killing the mother. If we valued mental health equivalently to human life we might feel able to advise him to take that drastic step (provided that he could get away with it). This is a conclusion from which most of us would shrink. In the last resort it is hard to accept that mental health or physical health or any *social* good is a value quite equivalent to human life.[58]

Christian ethics cannot accept abortion for reasons of "psychological health."

What about deformed fetuses? That wrenching dilemmas lie behind this question is painfully clear to anyone who has observed parents with severely deformed children. Nor are the social costs of care for the handicapped negligible. But can a society morally decide to eliminate persons because their care would be inconvenient or costly? Does greater affluence matter more than human beings? And if it is permissible to kill deformed fetuses, why is it not equally acceptable to kill those who are normal at birth but subsequently become seriously handicapped? "And what will prevent us from enlarging our definition of 'deformity' as a pretext for eliminating all 'undesirables' from society?"[59] Nazi-type social experiments and genocide lurk down this road.

Pregnancies resulting from rape and incest pose perhaps the most wrenching dilemmas of all. Anyone with a beloved daughter senses the agony of nine months of pregnancy for a rapist's vicious violation. Anyone sensitive to the long history of male abuse of women in both rape and incest feels the strength of the case for abortion in such situations. On the other hand, one dare not forget cases like that of the famous gospel singer Ethel Waters, whose life resulted from the rape of her mother at the age of thirteen.[60]

Most crucial, however, is the fact that the unborn child is also a human being created in God's image. When we weigh the shame, pain and inconvenience of the mother against the life of the unborn, how can abortion be acceptable? We dare not kill one human being because someone else has done wrong. Certainly redoubled efforts to provide loving care for women in such agonizing dilemmas is essential. So is a much more vigorous attack on male exploitation and abuse. But murder of the innocent is not the solution.

I conclude that abortion is morally acceptable only in the very exceptional cases when the physical life of the mother is threatened. What programs and policies in church and society should we then promote?

Chapter 3

Abortion and Public Policy

Abortion is "the great modern sin."[1]
Karl Barth

*O*n March 9, 1986, the National Organization of Women, the National Abortion Rights Action League and a host of other groups sponsored the "March for Women's Lives." Eighty-five thousand people, predominantly white, middle-class women, marched to champion abortion rights. Under the banner of "choice," the marchers chanted, "Not the church, not the state, women must decide their fate."

This slogan captures a central impulse of the movement. In a pluralistic democracy where people of good will differ, many argue that public policy should offer the maximum amount of liberty to all concerned. One person may believe life begins at conception, another at implantation, still another at birth, and some at some time after birth. With such a caldron of opinions, we should not, it is alleged, dictate a monolithic public policy.

This was essentially the view in the Roe vs. Wade decision, which legalized abortion. Justice Harry Blackmun, author of the opinion, argued that states with antiabortion laws elevated "one theory of life above all others."[2] Blackmun believed the Supreme Court decision was a neutral one. "Blackmun perceived the abortion debate as a clash between those who dogmatically insist that human life begins at conception and those who regard life's beginnings as an impenetrable mystery," writes Douglas Badger. "To leave the abortion decision to each individual appeared to him as a way not to take sides. Those who believe fetuses to be human need not procure abortions; those who believe that they are not, or that they become human at some advanced stage of pregnancy, are free to obtain abortions safely and legally."[3]

Governor Mario Cuomo of New York agrees. In a famous speech on abortion, personal faith and public policy, delivered in 1984 at Notre Dame University, Cuomo argued: "To assure our freedom we must allow others the same freedom, even if occasionally it produces conduct by them which we would hold to be sinful."[4] Cuomo added: "I protect my right to be a Catholic by preserving your right to be a Jew, a Protestant, or non-believer, or anything else you choose. We know that the price of seeking to force our beliefs on others is that they might someday force theirs on us."[5]

Why a Public Policy?

Unfortunately, the problem is not so easily solved. Both Justice Blackmun's and Governor Cuomo's positions are fundamentally problematic. In many kinds of situations neutrality by the state in the face of competing perspectives is precisely the right course. But that is totally unacceptable and unworkable when the issue is life itself. Honest conviction and sincere belief are not adequate grounds for taking the life of another person. Early Canaanite religion truly and sincerely believed in child sacrifice. Today, occult worshipers honestly affirm the rightness of ritual sacrifice. Some contemporary thinkers truly believe that a baby should not be treated as a human being until it demonstrates certain minimal ability. Others believe that the severely handicapped should be starved to death.

If society were to remain neutral and allow people who honestly believe that a certain category of person is rightly killed to implement their sincerely held beliefs, there would be chaos. Furthermore, such a situation would be morally intolerable to those who believe in the almost infinite significance of every person.

Governor Cuomo correctly points to the religious roots of the abortion question. But then he confuses the issue in a most unhelpful way. It is true that our ethical beliefs are finally grounded in our deepest religious convictions. Therefore, it is inevitable that differing views about the fetus flow ultimately from different religious perspectives.

But that does not mean that the person who believes abortion is murder and therefore demands a public policy that prevents abortion will therefore proceed to use the state to impose on everyone his or her views on adultery or the deity of Christ. Cuomo implies that if we are not "pro-choice," then we are violating the separation of church and state and ignoring other people's rights to be a Jew or Muslim or whatever. That is confusing nonsense. Insisting that the state take a stand on the general moral principle of the sanctity of all human life is not the same as demanding that the state legislate for or against specific religious dogmas.

I believe that all people should be free to believe and worship as they please. I also believe that people should be free to act in ways that I consider ethically wrong. But there is at least one important restriction on this freedom that every just society must maintain. My religious and ethical freedom does not include the right to kill other people.

Except in the case of abortion, nobody argues that one person should be free to take the life of another merely because the first person truly believes that the other person is not truly human. If the argument of the last chapter is valid, then we must act on the assumption that unborn babies and handicapped newborns are truly human. Therefore, abortion and infanticide are murder. In a pluralistic society people should be free to do many things that others consider stupid or sinful. But tolerance toward others does not extend to allowing them to kill other people.

At the same time, however, the pro-life movement must show understanding and respect for divergent views. Many people genuinely believe that the fetus, the handicapped newborn and the retarded infant are not human beings. Therefore, they believe that disposing of these lives is morally acceptable. Calling such persons murderers is just as unacceptable as calling a politician or general who truly believes in peace through strength a warmonger.[6]

On the other hand, in a pluralistic society "pro-choice" advocates should not expect people who deeply believe that abortion is murder to be satisfied with laws which permit abortion. Society has no obligation or even right to grant citizens freedom to kill others, even if they deny that such action is murder. The daily death of more than four thousand babies in abortion clinics in the United States alone is an outrage that must end.[7]

Wise, faithful activity to outlaw abortion, however, does not mean an all-or-nothing approach. Outlawing all abortions in the immediate future is politically impossible. Therefore, as Kenneth Kantzer has argued in a *Christianity Today* editorial, we should join others to write as soon as possible a less than perfect law that would outlaw many abortions.[8] Later, we can work for a still better law.

Those who believe abortion is wrong should work to reshape public policy in two ways. First, we must end most, if not all, abortions. And second, we should make abortion less attractive. We work at the first agenda through constitutional amendments and legislation which focus on the personhood or humanity of the unborn child. We do the second by making monogamy, family life and sexual responsibility more attractive.

James Skillen correctly insists that we go beyond the narrowly individualistic perspective of much "pro-choice" discussion. "The unborn are not separate, independent entities that can be approached outside the context of male and female sexual partnership. Unborn human beings are both the consequence of, and the possibility for, sexual intercourse, marriages, families, and all other human communities. The public legal question, therefore, is ... more broadly about the identity of the pregnant woman and father of the unborn in the context of human generations."[9]

Both grassroots activity and legislative activity are necessary simultaneously. Education, nurture and persuasion must come from the grassroots, while legislative efforts come from the top. Pressure must be felt from both directions. The success of the Civil Rights Movement followed this pattern. While thousands of Blacks and Whites marched in Selma and Montgomery, civil rights action was debated in Congress. When Bull Connor's dogs attacked children and when firemen hosed down old women, a recalcitrant Congress felt the heat and saw the light.

Constitutional Approaches to Stopping Abortion

There are only three ways in which any Supreme Court ruling can be reversed. First, the Supreme Court could overturn its decision in a subsequent ruling. Second, the President could try to change the number of members of the Supreme Court so he could "stack" it with justices who affirm the sanctity of human life. Third, Article 5 of the United States Constitution provides two possible ways to initiate a constitutional amendment: it can be proposed by a two-thirds vote in the House and Senate or by a constitutional convention authorized by two-thirds of the state legislatures. In either case, the proposed constitutional amendment must be ratified by three-fourths of the state legislatures.

The first is not impossible. The Court has reversed itself on over one-hundred-twenty different occasions. We have amended the Constitution only twenty-three times. The current court clearly will not reverse itself. On June 20, 1983, however, when the Court reaffirmed its Roe vs. Wade decision in Akron vs. Akron Center for Reproductive Health, Justice Sandra Day O'Connor issued a sharp dissent warning that "the Roe framework is clearly on a collision course with itself."[10] If two Supreme Court justices were replaced by persons who agreed with O'Connor, Court-permitted abortion on demand would end.

In 1937 Franklin Roosevelt attempted to reorganize the Court with his Judiciary Reorganization Bill. This effort was viewed as "packing" the Court with justices favorable to Roosevelt's policies by both Congress and the press. Given the delicate balance of powers in the federal government, it is likely that such a move would meet a similar fate today.

In the late seventies and early eighties there was a strong move to call a constitutional convention to draft an antiabortion amendment. Twenty of the necessary thirty-four states needed to call a convention agreed, but efforts to obtain the approval of fourteen more failed.

The other route to restoring the right to life to the unborn by a constitutional amendment is via an amendment approved by two-thirds of the U.S. House and Senate. One day after the Roe vs. Wade decision, evangelical Senator Mark Hatfield introduced a Human Life Amendment. Since then a host of amendments have been proposed. I will address only the two most widely discussed. The amendment preferred by most pro-life activists is known as the Unity Human Life Amendment. The text reads as follows:

Section 1. The right to life is the paramount and most fundamental right of a person.

Section 2. With respect to the right to life guaranteed to persons by the fifth and fourteenth articles of amendment to the Constitution, the word "person" applies to all human beings, irrespective of age, health, function, or condition of dependency, including their unborn offspring at every stage of their biological development including fertilization.

Section 3. No unborn person shall be deprived of life by any person: Provided, however, that nothing in this article shall prohibit a law allowing justification to be shown for only those medical procedures required to prevent the death of either the pregnant woman or her unborn offspring, as long as such law requires every reasonable effort be made to preserve the life of each.

Section 4. Congress and the several States shall have power to enforce this article by appropriate legislation.

This measure would affirm a constitutional right to life for all human beings regardless of age, health, function or condition of dependency, including unborn children from the moment of conception. This amendment would allow abortion to save the life of the mother so long as every reasonable effort is made to save the life of both mother and child.

A similar amendment known as the Garn-Oberstar Human Life Amendment was first introduced in 1974, and also enjoys wide pro-life support. It reads:

Section 1. With respect to the right to life, the word "person," as used in this article and in the fifth and fourteenth articles of amendment to the Constitution of the United States, applies to all human beings, irrespective of age, health, function, or condition of dependency, including their unborn offspring at every stage of their biological development.

Section 2. No unborn person shall be deprived of life by any person. Provided, however, that nothing in this article shall prohibit a law permitting only those medical procedures required to prevent the death of the mother.

Section 3. Congress and the several states shall have the power to enforce this article by appropriate legislation within their respective jurisdictions.[11]

Although the process is slow and the outcome uncertain, there is considerable merit in this long process. If the Supreme Court suddenly reversed itself, many women accustomed to the "right" of abortion would perhaps still seek illegal abortions. The legal process of passing a constitutional amendment, however, is an educational, consciousness-raising process. In fact, my own initial doubts about the validity of abortion occurred in just this way as I read (more than a decade ago) Senator Hatfield's defense of his proposed constitutional amendment. With a constitutional amendment, we must convince not just five Supreme Court justices, and not just two-thirds of the Congress, but also a majority of American citizens that abortion is wrong. Every legislative battle in every state would also be part of the process of developing a new public morality that rejects abortion.[12] Those who believe in the sanctity of human life need to work hard for a constitutional amendment of this kind. Given the current composition of Congress, of course, it is unlikely that any constitutional amendments will be passed in the near future. Thus other legislative restrictions are also important.

Statutory Measures

Several members of Congress have introduced legislation which would not only restrict abortion funding, but also challenge the Court's decisions on abortion.

The first such proposal, known as the Human Life Bill (HLB), was introduced in January 1981. The legal genius behind the bill, attorney Stephen Galebach, argued that in the same way Congress could enforce and interpret laws regarding literacy, so it could act in regard to the Roe vs. Wade decision.

Galebach argued that Congress is "co-enforcer," along with the courts, of the Fourteenth Amendment, which guards individuals against deprivation of life by states. Section 5 of that amendment provides that "Congress shall have the power to enforce, by appropriate legislation, the provisions of this article."

Galebach noted that Congress has in the past used this section as a basis for legislation crafted to dismantle Supreme Court decisions. In 1959, for example, the high court ruled that literacy tests, used by many states to deny minority citizens the right to vote, were constitutional. Six years later, Congress countered with the Voting Rights Act of 1965. Using powers conferred on it by section 5 of the Fourteenth Amendment, Congress found literacy tests employed in several Southern states, as well as similar tests administered to Hispanics in New York, to be discriminatory and proscribed their use. The effect was to overturn the Court's 1959 edict. Similarly, Congress can find that the Court erred in Roe vs. Wade and Doe vs. Bolton when it ruled that the unborn were not persons enjoying the safeguards of the Fifth and Fourteenth Amendments of the Constitution.[13]

The text of the first proposed version of the Human Life Bill is as follows:

Section 1. (a) The Congress finds that the life of each human being begins at conception. (b) The Congress further finds that the fourteenth amendment to the Constitution of the United States protects all human beings.

Section 2. Upon the basis of these findings, and in the exercise of the powers of Congress, including its power under section 5 of the fourteenth amendment to the Constitution of the United States, the Congress hereby recognizes that for the purpose of enforcing the obligation of the States under the fourteenth amendment not to deprive persons of life without due process of law, each human life exists from conception, without regard to race, sex, age, health, defect, or condition of dependency, and for this purpose "person" includes all human beings.

Section 3. Congress further recognizes that each State has a compelling interest, independent of the status of unborn children under the fourteenth amendment, in protecting the lives of those within the State's jurisdiction who the State rationally regards as human beings.

The heart of the HLB is the assertion that "the life of each human being begins at conception" and that the unborn are legal persons under the due process clause of the Fourteenth Amendment. According to the Senate Judiciary Committee's Subcommittee on

Separation of Powers, which held hearings on the measure, the HLB would compel the Supreme Court to review its rulings on the abortion cases. If the Supreme Court upheld its rulings, states would still be permitted (but not required) to restrict abortion. The bill was approved by the committee in 1981, but never came before the full Senate.

A similar measure was introduced in September 1982. This bill included nonbinding "findings" that the life of an individual human being begins at conception and that the Supreme Court "erred" in denying legal protection to the unborn. It further provided for the expedited Supreme Court review of any state statute passed on the basis of the act, thus creating a mechanism which would encourage the Court to review its 1973 ruling. This bill was filibustered and eventually tabled by a single vote.

Another measure, the Respect for Human Life Act, was introduced in the 1983 Congress. This act would permanently bar all forms of federal funding for abortion, except to save the mother's life.

Funding Measures: The Hyde Amendment

Immediately after the 1973 abortion decision, the Department of HEW (today HHS) began to pay for elective abortions through the Medicaid program. By 1976 the federal government was paying for 300,000 abortions on request annually.

That same year Congress adopted the Hyde Amendment, sponsored by Representative Henry Hyde of Illinois, which prohibited Medicaid funding of abortions except to save the mother's life. Since the Hyde Amendment was attached to an appropriations bill that pertained to only one fiscal year, this amendment must be passed every year. Similar "riders" have also been used to restrict the funding of military and Peace Corps volunteer abortions. Military abortion funding has now been prohibited by statutory law, which does not require annual renewal. Congress should enact the Hyde Amendment as a permanent statutory measure so that annual appropriations battles need not take place. Until May of 1981, advocates of abortion funding were able to establish certain "exceptions" which permitted the funding of abortions in cases of rape, incest and fetal disability. The only exception that exists today is the life of the mother.

Injunctions against the Hyde Amendment were issued by lower federal courts on several occasions between 1976 and 1980. On June 30, 1980, in Harris vs. McRae the Supreme Court ruled that the Hyde Amendment was constitutional. "It simply does not follow," the Court stated, "that a woman's freedom of choice carries with it a constitutional entitlement to the financial resources to avail herself of the full range of protected choices."[14]

The Hyde Amendment does not apply to the states, and so in spite of its passage, several states continue to fund abortion. Some fund essentially any request for abortion, while others supply funding only to save the life of the mother. Still others also fund abortion in the cases of rape and incest. State funding of abortion should be curbed as much as possible and the funds spent instead on programs which enhance human life instead of destroying it.

Other Means of Curbing Abortion
Health Insurance Measures. The group health insurance plans of many federal employees include mandatory coverage of abortion. In 1983 Congress prohibited the use of federal funds to provide abortion coverage for these plans, except to save the life of the mother. This measure, called the Smith/Denton Amendment or the Ashbrook Amendment, is not a part of statutory law and needs to be re-enacted annually.

Some states also require that health insurance plans with maternity benefits also cover abortion. In these states, legislation is needed that allows insurance policies to be bought and sold which provide maternity benefits only and do not pay for elective abortions. This gives the individual freedom not to purchase a policy which provides abortion coverage. The same policy should apply to health maintenance organizations.

There have also been attempts on Capitol Hill to establish "unisex" insurance policies which would make distinctions on the basis of sex within insurance policies illegal. According to many legal scholars, the effect would be to require elective abortion coverage within health insurance plans. Pregnancy would be viewed as an "ailment" to be treated either by surgical abortion or by carrying to term. Such legislation should be amended so that the consumer can request maternity benefits without abortion coverage. Thus abortion would be segregated as a deviant practice.

Parental Notification/Consent. On July 2, 1979, in Belloti vs. Baird,[15] the Supreme Court struck down a Massachusetts law that said an unmarried minor must have the consent of both parents before undergoing an abortion. The court decided that if the courts found the minor "mature" or found that an abortion would be "in her best interests," then the courts could authorize her to act without parental consultation or consent.

In a subsequent ruling (H. L. vs. Matheson, 23 Mar. 1981) the Court upheld a Utah statute requiring a physician to "notify, if possible" the parents or guardian of a minor before performing an abortion. The ruling was limited and applies only to dependent, unemancipated minors making no claims to maturity.

Local parental notification laws do have a positive impact and do save lives. Some justices routinely authorize abortions for minors, but others do not. Such laws do give pause to many minors. A girl may conclude that it is easier in the end to notify her parents rather than go through the court proceedings, which may in the end require that her parents be notified. Once parents and daughter begin to dialog, unexpected acceptance and new options often emerge.

Polls consistently show overwhelming support for parental consent legislation. Proposing it engages abortion proponents in debate and demonstrates how their agenda sometimes militates against the integrity of the family.

Conscience Clauses. Another way to work against abortion is to assure to the greatest degree possible that hospitals and hospital personnel have the right to refuse to perform, assist or accommodate abortion in any manner. Since 1973 and 1977, when the Supreme Court ruled that hospitals need not perform abortions, many private and public hospitals have acted accordingly. To date, forty-four states have passed legislation protecting the rights of conscience of hospital personnel, but compliance needs to be monitored and enforced.

ERA and Abortion. For years advocates of the Equal Rights Amendment have argued that there is no connection between abortion and the ERA. Logically there should not be. Nevertheless, pro-life political scholars have feared that state and federal ERAs, as currently worded, would be interpreted in a manner which would require public funding of abortion and nullify conscience clauses.

Their fears are not unfounded. Already, American Civil Liberties Union (ACLU) attorneys have urged the courts in four states to rule that the restrictions of state funding for elective abortions discriminates on the basis of sex, thus violating state ERAs. On March 9, 1984, the Commonwealth Court of Pennsylvania ruled that two state laws which restricted Medicaid funding of elective abortion were discriminatory based on the state ERA. The court said the ERA was "sufficient in and of itself to invalidate the statutes before us [restricting funding of elective abortions] in that those statutes do unlawfully discriminate against women with respect to a physical condition unique to women."[16] Similar arguments are being considered in other states in order to defend Medicaid funding of abortion.

Consequently, many constitutional scholars assert that the federal courts would likely interpret the federal ERA in the same manner. It is essential, therefore, to add an "abortion-neutralization" amendment to the ERA as it is currently worded, since the

ERA might otherwise invalidate any law which "discriminates" against abortion. This would eliminate both funding restrictions and also conscience laws which protect medical personnel who refuse to participate in abortion.

A widely accepted "abortion-neutralization" amendment reads as follows: "Nothing in this article [the ERA] shall be construed to grant or secure any right relating to abortion or the funding thereof." With the inclusion of this statement, the ERA would be an important affirmation of the rights of women.

Unfortunately, "abortion rights" are firmly entrenched in the agenda of a major part of the feminist lobby. (This, however, is not true of Feminists for Life of America, which is a forum for women's-rights activists who support ERA but oppose abortion.[17]) This was demonstrated on November 15, 1983, when the ERA was brought to the House floor under an extraordinary procedure which did not permit the abortion-neutralization amendment. ERA was defeated because of this. The ERA has not come up in the House again because its supporters are aware that the House has the necessary votes to attach the amendment. Apparently, they would rather not have the ERA at all if it contains a rider which neutralizes its relevance to abortion rights.[18]

Fetal Experimentation. One grisly practice that has grown up around the abortion industry is experimentation on fetuses. Infants who survive abortions are sometimes used as experimental subjects. And some children slated for abortion have nontherapeutic experiments performed on them. For example, researchers inject drugs and chemicals and then examine the effects after the child dies. Legislation is necessary to stop these barbaric practices. Federal regulations limit the use of federal funds for nontherapeutic fetal experimentation, but two-thirds of the states permit these practices to continue unchecked.[19]

Wrongful Life/Wrongful Birth
Wrongful life/birth suits are those where either parents or chil-

dren claim that the child's life was wrongfully allowed to continue or came about due to negligence. The assumption is that had the parents known the mother was carrying a defective child she would have had an abortion. Implicit in this is the contention that the disabled child does not have a life worth living.

In addition to promoting an unacceptable view of human life, these suits encourage doctors to recommend abortion in many instances for fear of incurring lawsuits if they do not. Minnesota and South Dakota have passed legislation stating that no one may file a suit against another on the basis that their action or inaction caused a child to be wrongfully born. These laws protect physicians from suits because they did not recommend abortion. These laws not only protect the lives of unborn children with possible handicaps, they also reject the ghastly notion that parents have a positive duty to execute such children.[20]

Baby Doe Legislation. Besides measures designed to curb abortion, Christian citizens should also monitor legislation to prohibit infanticide. In April of 1982 a newborn with Downs syndrome and an incomplete esophagus (which is treatable by routine surgery) was allowed to starve to death in six days at the request of his parents and the sanction of the Indiana courts. This celebrated instance of infanticide led to the introduction of federal regulations by the Department of Health and Human Services to protect "Baby Does," as they came to be known. When the regulations were sidetracked by court injunctions, legislation was passed by Congress during the summer of 1984. The law became part of the Child Abuse Act and defined denial of routine medical care, food and water as child abuse. State child-abuse agencies were assigned the task of monitoring, identifying and protecting potential victims of infanticide. Individual states need to pass legislation to protect "Baby Does." Citizens need to make sure child-abuse agencies follow up on reports of medical neglect.

Contrary to the contentions of the American Medical Association and other opponents of the law, the measure did not require useless medical treatment in hopeless cases. Rather, it protected handicapped newborns from lethal discrimination because of actual or potential impairments. Virtually all handicapped advocacy groups, including the Association for Retarded Citizens and the Spina Bifida Association, supported the legislation.[21]

On June 9, 1986, the Supreme Court struck down the Baby Doe regulations, stating that the federal government cannot force hospitals to treat severely handicapped infants over the objections of their parents. The Court further ruled that federal oversight and investigative powers under the regulations were impermissible. Last October, however, new regulations were issued which require states to call on child protective services to investigate possible abuses in the treatment of handicapped infants. To date, these regulations have not been challenged in court since they are significantly weaker than the previous ones. Disability-rights organizations will most likely press for legislation which would make medical judgments regarding the treatment of handicapped infants subject to federal law. Pro-life citizens should support such legislation and make certain that child protective agencies are investigating potential abuses.

Government-Funded Educational Campaign. Developing a pro-life outlook is mainly the responsibility of the family and religious institutions. But a carefully constructed government information campaign could help. Today government programs warn citizens about the evils of smoking and alcohol abuse. A similar program on abortion would include publicly funded billboards against abortion and spot ads on TV and radio. Educational programs in the schools would discourage adolescent sexual activity by fostering self-esteem and self-control as an essential component of personal maturity and social responsibility.

Providing Alternatives to Abortion
Women—especially poor, single women—often feel that they have no alternative to abortion. It is to the credit of the Christian

Action Council and other pro-life Christians that they have worked hard to develop a large number of Crisis Pregnancy Centers. But that by itself is not enough. The integrity of the pro-life movement depends on its vigorously supporting changes in public policy that give women and families additional meaningful alternatives. The following are especially important: expanded research on nonabortive, reliable, safe methods of family planning; assistance for programs supporting women who carry children to term; vigorous prosecution of sexual violence against women; expanded services and schooling for disabled children; support for programs to make available better opportunities in education, jobs and housing to poor people so that they no longer feel they have to choose between desperate poverty and abortion.

Male responsibility for children must increase. Pregnancy continues to be a largely female responsibility partly because males abdicate their role as fathers. We could foster increased male responsibility in many ways. Making paternity suits more accessible to women would help. So would stronger child support enforcement and tighter divorce laws. As I point out at greater length in chapter seven, women, not men, have been the economic losers with no-fault divorce laws. Funding for research to discover a safe, reliable male contraceptive so that men share the responsibility for pregnancy prevention is also important.

Funding should increase for crisis pregnancy centers, adoption agencies, prenatal and teen health clinics, and agencies that teach parenting skills and prevent prematurity. The extended family should also be empowered to be able to support an unplanned pregnancy.

Adoption also needs to become a more attractive option. We should modernize adoption laws which arbitrate and advocate the rights, needs and concerns of the birth parents, adoptive parents and adoptive children. Educational efforts to remove the stigma attached to adoption are needed. Adoption is a loving act for the child and a wonderful way to build families. We also need to encourage people to adopt across traditional barriers.[22]

Space limitations prevent an adequate discussion of all the needed measures. Some are discussed later in this book. As Just-Life, a new consistently pro-life political action committee, insists, pro-life activists should be equally concerned with the negative task of restricting abortions and the positive task of promoting alternatives. After stating its vigorous stand against abortion, Just-Life's Statement of Philosophy continues:

> JustLife believes with equal conviction that government should support programs that offer meaningful alternatives to abortion for pregnant women and their families. The readily available option of abortion as a tool of social policy encourages society to evade its obligation to attack the unjust structures and conditions that encourage some to seek abortion: poverty, sexism, lack of adequate health care, sexual abuse, and ignorance about birth control information. Many women have virtually no reasonable choice.

> JustLife demands that society provide other options than either the trauma of abortion or motherhood without adequate support. JustLife therefore believes that a consistent pro-life stance will insist that government should promote programs that offer adequate health care, needed child care, economic support, assistance for the families of disabled children, and adoption alternatives. Women must be able to make a responsible decision against abortion without losing all opportunity for fulfilled lives. Only when government policy truly promotes this goal is it genuinely and consistently pro-life.

Pro-life activists have sometimes been accused of acting as if "life begins at conception and ends at birth." There is a clear—albeit costly—way to refute this charge. It is to work as hard for pro-life programs designed to guarantee quality of life to the already living as we work for policies that will ensure life itself to the not yet born. That ought to be the acid test of the moral integrity and biblical validity of the pro-life movement.

Part 2

ECONOMICS

Chapter 4

Both Justice and Freedom

The needs of the poor take priority over the desires of the rich; the rights of workers over the maximization of profits; the preservation of the environment over uncontrolled industrial expansion; production to meet social needs over production for military purposes.[1]
John Paul II

Millions today die needlessly from starvation and malnutrition. A billion lie trapped in grinding poverty. Part of their tragedy is due to economic structures that are unfair. One crucial test of the integrity of the pro-life movement will be its attitude toward public policies that ignore the poverty of a billion troubled neighbors.

That God cares about economics is clear to anyone who reads the Bible carefully. It is probably the second most frequent topic in the Scriptures. This chapter contains a brief outline of some of the central biblical themes that relate to shalom and the economic realm: the importance and purpose of work; God's special concern for the poor; the rejection of great extremes of wealth and poverty; and the importance of and limitations on private property.[2]

The Glory of Work
To be human is to work.[3] God created men and women to be co-

shapers of history. As we respectfully till the garden which God has entrusted to our care, we accept this divine invitation and experience an important part of the fullness of life intended by the Creator.

The summons to work is intimately connected with the fact that we are created in the divine image. The Genesis story portrays God at work for six vigorous days before he rests from his labor on the sabbath. When God becomes flesh, we see him sawing and pounding year after year at the carpenter's bench.

Work, at its best, is the way each person expresses his or her uniqueness and individuality. When working conditions squelch or prevent this purpose of work, they obstruct God's intention.

Work is also the way we obey the divine command to care for ourselves and our families (2 Thess 3:12; 1 Tim 5:8). Even some elements of Israelite relief efforts (for example, gleaning in the fields after the harvesters) required personal initiative, responsibility and work on the part of those helped. Those who, because of laziness, refuse the summons to work despise both the example and command of the Creator.

Finally, work is the way we demonstrate our love for neighbor. Created to live in community in interdependence on others, we work to help shape a world where the labor of each enriches the life of all.

The U.S. Catholic bishops rightly conclude that this biblical perspective on work has clear implications for the shape of a just economic order: "It should enable persons to find a significant measure of self-realization in their labor; it should permit persons to fulfill their material needs through adequate remuneration; and it should make possible the enhancement of unity and solidarity within the family, the nation and the world community."[4]

God and the Poor
God reveals a special concern for the poor in every part of the Scriptures—both Old Testament and New, prophetic writings and

wisdom literature, the Gospels and Epistles. Constantly the Scriptures insist that this special concern for the poor and oppressed is central to the very nature of God (Ps 146). "He who is kind to the poor lends to the LORD" (Prov 19:17). "The LORD . . . executes justice for the needy" (Ps 140:12). Jesus' preaching to the poor is central to his Messianic mission and evidence that he is the Messiah (Lk 4:16-21 and 7:18-23). God warns the rich to weep and howl because of impending divine punishment for their neglect and mistreatment of the poor (Jas 5:1-5).

In some basic sense God is on the side of the poor. Also, in a sense, God is not on the side of the rich. That is not to say God is biased; Scripture explicitly denies divine bias (Job 34:8-19; Deut 10:17-19). God cares equally about everyone and demands economic justice for all. The overwhelming majority of rich and powerful folk in all societies past and present, however, care much more for their own well-being than for that of the poor. Corrupted by the Fall, they use the levels of power in society for their own selfish advantage. God, by contrast, is truly unbiased and thus cares equally about everyone. Hence in comparison to the actions of the rich and powerful, God appears to have a powerful bias toward the poor. God sides with the poor precisely in the sense that because he is unbiased he demands economic justice for all.

But why are people poor? Some people offer the simplistic answer that all poverty results from economic oppression by the rich. That is nonsense. The Bible is realistic. Some poverty results from laziness, or sinful choices about drugs or alcohol (Prov 6:6-11; 19:15; 20:13). Some poverty results from religious systems that do not encourage initiative, work and creativity. Obviously evangelism, repentance and conversion are central to the solution of such poverty.

Many people, on the other hand, rationalize their own affluence in the face of widespread poverty by blaming the poor for their own misery. Laziness, sinful choices or a failure to take advantage of available technology is used to allegedly explain most poverty. This is not the biblical perspective. Although the Scriptures occasionally blame the poor for their poverty, far more often they attribute it to oppression by the rich and powerful:

> The LORD enters into judgment with the elders and princes of his people: "It is you who have devoured the vineyard, the spoil of the poor is in your houses." (Is 3:14)

Or Jeremiah 5:27:

> Like a basket full of birds, their houses are full of treachery; therefore, they have become great and rich, they have grown fat and sleek.

God's attitude toward such rich folk is very clear and explicit. God abhors their oppression and pulls down their houses and societies (Is 3:14-25; Jer 22:13-19; Is 10:1-3). And he hates their worship (Amos 5:21-24; Is 58:3-8).

The Scriptures even raise the most serious doubt about whether such people even know or love God at all (Jer 22:16; 1 Jn 3:17-18). Precisely because God cares equally for all, he punishes individuals and societies that oppress the poor.

Any approach to the whole area of economics that fails to emphasize God's overwhelming concern for economic justice for the poor is simply unbiblical.

Extremes of Wealth and Poverty

Another important clue about the nature of economic justice comes from the biblical teaching that God condemns extremes of wealth and poverty. Sinful people may well selfishly develop greater and greater extremes between rich and poor. Among the redeemed, however, God demands transformed economic relationships.

After Israel entered Canaan, the land was divided more or less equally (Num 26:52-56). God wanted tribes and families to have enough to earn their own way. Then God added the provision for a Jubilee every fifty years (Lev 25). Every fiftieth year all land was to return to the original owners—without compensation and without questions asked about possible failures on the part of the poor folk who had lost their land. Deuteronomy 15 added the demand that every seven years all debts must be forgiven. Both measures were divinely willed societal mechanisms to prevent ever greater extremes between the wealthy and the poor and to move society in the direction of equality of economic opportunity.

It is important to see that the Jubilee passage also teaches personal responsibility. Those who make wrong decisions and lose their land do not get it back immediately—in fact, in many cases they would not get it back during their lifetime! They must live with the consequences of their actions until the next Jubilee. On the other hand, the restoration of land every fifty years works against an ever-increasing centralization of wealth. It fosters a basic equality of economic opportunity for all, at least to the degree that all have the means to earn the basic necessities of life.

This concern for redeemed economic relationships among the people of God did not end with the Old Testament. Jesus talked frequently about the way his followers would share with the poor (Mt 25:31-40). Filled with the Holy Spirit, the first church obeyed Christ's teachings so dramatically and shared so thoroughly that "there was not a needy person among them" (Acts 4:34). And the apostle Paul, the great missionary to the Gentiles, considered economic fellowship in the body of Christ so important that he devoted hours and hours of potential preaching time to an interracial, intercontinental offering. He collected donations from Greek-speaking European Christians for Aramaic-speaking Asian Christians (2 Cor 8—9).

> I do not mean that others should be eased and you burdened, but that as a matter of equality your abundance at the present time should supply their want, so that their abundance may supply your want, that there may be equality. (2 Cor 8:13-14)

Neither the Jubilee provisions or the Pauline teaching on intercontinental sharing mean that God demands some wooden, absolutely egalitarian equality of consumption. But surely the texts demonstrate beyond any doubt that God desires an end to extremes of wealth and poverty among his people.

Nor does the principle apply only in the church. God did not impose arbitrary demands in the Bible. God's revealed norms were designed to guarantee social wholeness among the people of God. To the extent that any society implements the biblical principles disclosed by God to Israel and the church, greater wholeness will result.

Two important elements of economic justice, therefore, are the absence of extremes of wealth and poverty and the presence of equality of economic opportunity (at least with reference to the basic necessities of life). The doctrine of sin underlines why these principles are so important. Wealth is power. And power is dangerous. Because of the Fall, power tends to corrupt and absolute power tends to corrupt absolutely. Sinful, selfish people cannot be trusted to use great economic power for the common good rather than for themselves. Therefore, if freedom and economic justice for all are important goals, we will structure society to exhibit and overcome extremes of wealth and poverty.

That does not mean that economics is a zero-sum game where increasing my wealth automatically means that someone else loses. Hard work and technological invention can create new wealth for all. Not all differences in income result from sin, selfishness and greed. The biblical teaching on work and humanity's dominion over the earth affirms the goodness and importance of the creation of wealth.

Private Property
Scripture also supports the notion of private property. Both implicitly and explicitly, the Ten Commandments sanction private ownership (Ex 10:15, 17). Jesus apparently assumed its legitimacy—otherwise, his commands to give to the poor and loan to the needy would make no sense (Mt 6:2-4; 5:42; Lk 6:34-35).

Although the Bible affirms the validity of private property, it totally rejects any notion of absolute private ownership.[5] God is the only absolute owner. As Lord of all, God possesses unconditional property rights to every thing. "Whatever is under the whole heaven is mine" (Job 41:11; see also Ps 50:12; Deut 26:10). Because God alone is absolute owner, God can insist that the right of everyone to have land (so as to earn a living) is a higher right than some notion of unlimited, absolute private ownership. Hence we have God's demand that Israel practice Jubilee every fifty years: "The land shall not be sold in perpetuity, for the land is mine; for you are strangers and sojourners with me" (Lev 25:23).

Leviticus 25:25-28 contains another striking limitation on the rights of private ownership. Between the years of Jubilee, the land can be sold. However, if a poor person sells some land and then recovers financial solvency, the new owner must sell back the land even if he prefers to keep it. The original family's right to have their property in order to be able to earn their own way is a higher right than the new owner's right to maximize profits.

The Bible challenges any person or system devoted to absolutizing property rights. It also rejects any notion of state ownership of the major means of production. Leviticus 25 does not suggest either a vast permanent welfare system (which runs the great danger of promoting dependency) or state ownership (which leads to totalitarianism). In order to promote strong families able to earn their own way, Jubilee called for regular redistribution of the land. Since land was the basic capital in early Israel, that mechanism, if followed, would have promoted a decentralized form of limited private ownership where everyone had the economic resources to shape their own life and earn their own way. The Jubilee principle, someone has suggested, "esteems private property more highly than capitalism does, for it insists that no family be permanently without it."[6]

Decentralized, private ownership (understood as stewardship) rather than state ownership as in socialism and communism is important for both a positive and a negative reason. Positively, the biblical doctrine of creation summons each person to be a co-worker with God. God wants us to exercise dominion over the earth, shape history and genuinely influence the decisions that affect our lives. If economic power is centralized in state ownership, persons and families become cogs in complex economic machines. They are denied the freedom to shape the crucial decisions that affect their lives.

Negatively, as we have already noted, power tends to corrupt and absolute power tends to corrupt absolutely. Therefore, the centralization of economic power and political power in the same hands is exceedingly dangerous in a fallen world. As the highly repressive Communist society of the USSR demonstrates, this kind of centralization almost guarantees a totalitarianism that tramples on religious and political freedom. Decentralization of power is essential if liberty is to thrive.

It is astonishing, however, to see how inconsistently many people apply this principle about the danger of centralized economic power. Some denounce the danger in the case of totalitarian Communist societies and then fail to apply the same principle to Western societies where huge multinational corporations exercise immense economic and therefore enormous political influence. (For others, alas, the blindness is reversed!) So vast is the economic power of the five hundred largest corporations (and the few thousand people who control them) that genuine democracy is significantly undermined in North America and Western Europe. A biblically informed fear of concentrated power will demand changes in both East and West.

The preceding discussion has focused on several crucial components of a biblical perspective on economics:

First, work is essential to the nature of persons.

Second, God's special concern for justice for the poor must also be a central concern for God's people.

Third, reducing or preventing extremes of wealth and poverty and moving in the direction of equality of economic opportunity are essential for economic justice. Therefore, redistribution of resources so everyone can stand on their own feet and earn their own way is important.

Fourth, the creation of wealth is good and important, but it dare not become the ultimate goal or highest value.

Fifth, limited private ownership is good when understood as stewardship under God who is the only absolute owner. Centralized economic power, whether controlled by the state or by vast corporations, is dangerous and almost inevitably evil. We should therefore promote decentralized, private ownership, since this enables persons and families to earn their own way and be co-workers with God in the shaping of history.

Sixth, personal responsibility in the economic realm is also a biblical summons and people must live with the consequences of wrong economic decisions.

Finally, there is a significant connection between decentralized economic ownership and political and religious liberty. The biblical doctrine of sin explains the historical fact that centralized state ownership of most resources almost guarantees totalitarianism.

Tragically, we are all tempted to stress some of these principles and neglect others. But that leads to biblical one-sidedness. The Bible affirms both economic redistribution and the creation of wealth, both communal sharing and individual responsibility, both freedom and justice, both decentralized private ownership and social limitations on individual greed.

In the next chapter I will take up the urgent task of applying all these biblical principles to the complex world of modern economic life.

Chapter 5

On Implementing Justice

Those who defend the right to life of the weakest among us must be equally visible in support of the quality of life of the powerless among us: The old and the young, the hungry and the homeless, the undocumented immigrant and the unemployed worker. Such a quality of life posture translates into specific political and economic postures on tax policy, employment generation, welfare policy, nutrition and feeding programs, and health care.[1]
Cardinal Joseph Bernardin

Another possibility is that antiabortion people are not really interested in developing a [consistent] "pro-life" philosophy but rather are just using the "pro-life" label because it will enhance their political effectiveness.[2]
Donald Granberg

For many, the words *economic justice* evoke an image of poverty and starvation in the Third World. But poverty and economic injustice also exist in the United States. Yet to discuss public-policy options with even a minimum of depth for both the domestic and international arenas would be impossible in one short chapter. Since I have dealt with the international scene elsewhere,[3] this chapter will focus exclusively on the question of domestic economic justice.

At the end of 1983 about 15.2 per cent of the population—35 million people—were poor according to the U.S. government.[4] (In 1986 a nonfarm family of four is deemed poor if its income is less than $11,496.) Some poverty in the United States is short-term. It results from changes in family circumstances such as loss of a job, disability or illness. But a significant number of people are poor for long periods. This is particularly true for members of racial minorities, the elderly, children and those in families headed by women. Especially tragic is the worsening problem of poverty among children. In 1983, twenty-two per cent of Americans under the age of eighteen lived in poor families. Almost half of all black children and over half the children in families headed by women were below the poverty line.[5]

The physical effects of poverty are harsh even in the United States. The infant mortality rate has slowed its decline.[6] A 1983 survey by the Massachusetts Department of Public Health starkly demonstrated the effects of hunger among low-income children: nearly one-fifth were either stunted, abnormally under weight or anemic.[7] In March 1985 a task force of twenty-two physicians and public health experts reported that at least twenty million Americans go hungry at least two days a month. They also found instances of calorie and protein malnutrition that caused reduced birth weight and growth, listlessness and increased susceptibility to diseases not directly caused by hunger.[8]

Poverty in the United States is nothing like what it is in most of the world. (But ask any American middle-class family with at least two children how they would feel if they had to scrape by on only $11,486 a year!) And yet American poverty exists amidst one of the most unequal distributions of income and wealth in the Western industrialized world.[9] In 1984 the richest twenty per cent of Americans received forty-two per cent of the nation's after-tax income, while the poorest twenty per cent received only five per cent.[10] The distribution of wealth (as opposed to annual income) is even more unequal. The same top twenty per cent owned nearly eighty per cent of the nation's net wealth, while the bottom half owned just one per cent.[11] After remaining fairly stable for thirty years, the gap in the United States between rich and poor in terms of wealth and income has begun to grow in the 1980s.[12]

Unemployment continues to wreak havoc. Despite some recovery from the recession, 7.5% of the U.S. labor force was looking for work in 1984 but could not find it. Nor is the U.S. economy an equal opportunity unemployer. Women heading families had an unemployment rate of 10.3%; Blacks, 15.9%; and Black teenagers, 42.7%.[13]

In addition to the unemployed, millions of other people are underemployed. The underemployed work but do not earn enough to support themselves or their families. Their jobs frequently offer little hope of advancement. In the United States in 1983, two million people worked full-time for the entire year and still were poor.[14]

How can Christians effectively seek solutions to these economic problems? The basic direction of public policy flows fairly directly from the biblical principles developed in the last chapter. Government policy should promote full employment and a healthy, decentralized, private economy. We should respect private property and preserve private ownership of the means of production. But exclusive reliance on a laissez-faire market mechanism does not guarantee justice. Regardless of race, sex, age and religion, all persons should have equal opportunities to participate in the economy. Government should support quality education for all children and adults, especially those who are disadvantaged. These policies support human dignity and empower people by providing the skills needed to take control of their own lives and provide for their own needs.

Implementing these general guidelines, however, is not easy. Most public-policy issues require answers to complex questions of fact. How can we promote full employment and control inflation? Should the United States adopt an "industrial policy" to compete with foreign businesses who receive support from their governments? What are the causes of poverty in the United States today? How much results from sinful choices on the part of individuals?

How much from unfair economic structures? Must we sacrifice economic efficiency to promote a more just distribution of economic power and resources? In what sense are we running out of natural resources? On these important but penultimate questions Christians rightly may disagree. Thus I do not expect everyone to concur with the policy prescriptions that follow. They represent my best judgment, not the only "Christian" position.

As I insist throughout this book, Christians should not expect government to solve all our problems. Individual Christians should attempt to reduce economic injustice through their personal vocational activity, private agencies and the church. But good public policy is also crucial.

The state plays at least four important roles in the economy, and in these ways can work as an agent of justice. As rulemaker, it establishes the laws which govern private economic relations. As broker, it distributes economic power and resources within the private sector. As a participant in the economy, the government spends its tax revenues in many different ways, some of which have a direct effect on economic justice (public education, health programs, resource conservation to name a few). In fact, government is such an important participant in the economy that it assumes a fourth role, namely, influencing the health of the overall economy through its fiscal (for instance, taxing and spending) and monetary policies.

That government (as rulemaker) establishes the rules for the economy does not mean that it should prohibit all immoral economic behavior (for example, spending all of one's income on oneself without giving to the poor). Biblical principles of individual responsibility as well as modern Western legal principles of individual liberty (most notably, those in the U.S. Constitution) require limited government.

When the government as rulemaker and broker attempts to promote equality of economic opportunity, it must be extremely sensitive to the values of individual freedom. One person's freedom may be another person's enslavement. A powerful private entity, such as a large corporation, often can coerce weaker participants in the economy just as effectively as can government. To employees threatened with the loss of their jobs, it makes little difference that their employer lacks the sword of the state.[15] A free market, therefore, is not an absolute good that a democratically elected government dare never limit, but the promotion of equal economic opportunity so that all may participate in the economy is essential. This balance can be achieved by civil rights and antitrust laws, publicly financed education, job training and placement. Rather than subscribing to a rigid laissez-faire doctrine or demanding a totally egalitarian equality of economic consumption, government must balance the sometimes competing values of meeting basic needs, providing equal opportunities and preserving freedom.

Civil government cannot escape this role, even if it attempts to institute a pure laissez-faire system in which government regulation is minimal. The state necessarily has an effect on the conduct of economic activities and the economic welfare of its citizens. The only question is whether that effect will promote or undermine justice and other basic values. For example, federal laws insuring the rights of workers to bargain collectively have done much to improve the lot of millions of workers who would otherwise still be in a disadvantageous position in bargaining for wages and benefits with their employers. Government cannot be neutral about employer-employee relationships because civil law provides the very structure of those relationships. Doing away with federal collective bargaining laws might result in a return to traditional state laws governing the relationship (and favoring the employer), as they did during the period of frequently violent labor strife of the late nineteenth and early twentieth centuries.

Thus far my suggestions have been at a general, abstract level. But the problems of economic life are concrete. The solutions, therefore, must also be specific. Within the space of one chapter

I cannot set forth a detailed agenda for reshaping the total economic life of the nation. Instead I select two important areas of current economic debate—welfare reform and tax reform—to illustrate the direction in which I believe our society should move. How could the welfare system be changed so that it would empower the poor to stand on their own feet rather than create dependency? How could tax laws be more just?

Welfare Reform

Federal, state and local governments administer a number of programs which fall under the general category of "social welfare programs." Some explicitly supplement the market incomes of the poor. (Aid to Families with Dependent Children [AFDC], the largest program providing cash support to low-income families, is what most people refer to when they speak of welfare.) Others provide payments to members of specific groups such as the blind, disabled and aged, without regard to the income of the individual (Social Security). Others help make medical care available to the aged (Medicare) and poor (Medicaid). Still others make commodities available to the poor at low cost (food stamps; nutrition aid for women, infants and children; and public housing).

Most people agree that as a society we should assist the aged and disabled who are unable to support themselves. Many, but not all, would add to that list single parents with small children. In the case of the able-bodied without child-care responsibilities, however, there is far more disagreement. Many believe the welfare system reduces the incentive of recipients to work, fosters dependency on the public dole, and encourages divorce, separation and illegitimate births. Therefore, some have proposed its wholesale elimination.[16]

Current public-assistance programs are far from ideal. Yet many of the accusations contain unfair stereotypes of welfare recipients. And the critics usually fail to offer suggestions for constructive reform. Often, too, they ignore other problems: inadequate payment levels in some states, stigmatization of persons receiving assistance and the lack of incentives for people to move off welfare.[17] At the same time, no one should try to deny that the present welfare system is a disaster. It has created dependency. Fundamental reform is necessary.

The central goal of welfare policy should be to meet the basic needs of those unable to care for themselves in a way that empowers the poor to move toward self-sufficiency, avoids a cycle of dependency, and strengthens the institutions of marriage and the family. Obviously the poor cannot move toward self-sufficiency if there are no jobs for them. Therefore full employment is an indispensable element of any long-term solution to the problems of the welfare system. Basic values about sexuality, marriage and work also must change. (This is a long-term task which is primarily the responsibility of religious institutions, not the government.)

Frankly, I feel we currently lack the necessary far-reaching proposals for fundamentally changing the welfare system in ways that are consistent with biblical values. That is not to say that no proposed changes exist. Some favor wholesale slashing of welfare provisions.[18] Others demand that we blindly continue unsuccessful programs. What we desperately need is a new generation of biblical economists (as thoroughly committed to the poor as God is) who will work out genuinely new solutions. Although the details of such proposals are still unclear, the general direction we need to move is evident: we should redistribute resources so that the poor have genuine equality of economic opportunity to earn a decent living; we should demand personal responsibility, work and initiative; and we should strengthen the family.

Working out these new biblically shaped proposals will take time. So will the task of creating jobs for all and transforming basic values. Meanwhile, we dare not let people suffer desperate poverty. Four short-term changes would buy time for more far-reaching solutions.

First, a national minimum level of assistance would help implement the Christian conviction that the right to life means that no neighbor should be allowed to go without minimal food, clothing, shelter and medical care. Currently the combined benefits of AFDC and food stamps often amount to less than three-fourths of the official poverty line.[19] And because individual states have broad authority within federal guidelines to set benefit levels for AFDC, payments vary markedly among the states. (In 1983 a family of three received $530 per month in Vermont and $96 in Mississippi.[20]) We should rewrite federal guidelines to provide for a national minimum-benefit level, which states may supplement if they wish. Annual adjustments in this minimum amount should reflect increases in the cost of living. From 1972 to 1984, the combined value of AFDC and food-stamp benefits for a family of four with no other income fell an average of twenty-two per cent, mostly because so many states failed to increase benefit levels with inflation.[21]

Second, we should significantly modify the welfare system to encourage gainful employment for recipients who are able to work. Current programs discourage work because earnings from a job sharply reduce welfare payments. Today, AFDC benefits are reduced by one dollar for every dollar of earned income (after four months on the job, and after allowing for child care and other work-related expenses).[22] The implicit tax on such employment is therefore 100%. The law provides no financial incentive for trying to support oneself. (In fact, the implicit tax can be even greater than 100%. Accepting a job may make one ineligible for a program, such as Medicaid, worth hundreds of dollars.)

This was not always the case. From 1967 until 1981 the first thirty dollars of monthly earnings and one-third of any amount above that did not trigger a reduction in benefits. But Congress and the president eliminated this incentive in order to cut the budget and trim welfare rolls of all but the "truly needy." Many families with outside income suddenly found their benefits cut, sometimes to zero. Previously, for example, an AFDC mother of three earning $450 per month would have received a monthly benefit of $230 (in 1984 dollars). (Even then, she still was below the poverty line.) Now she would receive only $50. Employment of AFDC recipients is expected to decline as a result, although no data is yet available.[23]

Despite such disincentives, earnings from work still have accounted for a significant part of the total income of most welfare recipients, especially that majority who receive benefits for short periods of time. In one study of AFDC recipients, seven out of ten received less than fifty per cent of their total income from welfare during the time they received assistance. For more than half of them, welfare accounted for less than thirty per cent of their total income.[24] This suggests that most of the welfare population wants to work. Yet they are not blind to financial reality. If the welfare system penalizes work, they will not work. The little hard evidence that is available suggests that the lack of work incentives in public-assistance programs does reduce participation in the market economy.[25] We ought to quickly change the law so that it offers a financial incentive for people to work.

Recent experiments in several states, including Massachusetts, indicate that government can do even more to encourage welfare recipients to work. (Mothers with young children, of course, should be able to stay at home to care for them.) Previously, Massachusetts experimented with mandatory workfare (no work, no welfare), but that was a failure. Then in 1983, the state began an aggressive job-training and job-placement program for welfare recipients who wanted to work. To add incentive, recipients who gain jobs receive free child care for one year and Medicaid benefits for fifteen months. The results are striking. Massachusetts' case load is the lowest in twelve years.[26]

A third direction for welfare reform is to insure that it strengthens rather than weakens marriages and families. The hard evidence that welfare has led to family dissolution and illegitimacy is spotty.[27] One factor in the horrendous growth of one-parent families among the poor is that they have made many of the same sinful choices that other income groups have. They have accepted looser sexual mores, marital separation and divorce in the name of personal fulfillment. Welfare payments do not dictate these decisions. But they may make it easier for the poor to make the same mistakes that others do. Even more destructive for the family is the lack of opportunities for men to work at jobs with decent wages. This has destroyed both their ability to support their families and also their self-respect. Lack of jobs and inadequate wages are more important than welfare benefits in explaining the increase in families headed by women. In one study, a ten per cent rise in AFDC payments was accompanied by a two per cent rise in female-headed families. On the other hand, a ten per cent rise in male wage rates was associated with an eight per cent decline in such families.[28]

Welfare programs should treat two-parent families as favorably as single-parent families in otherwise identical circumstances. This probably will not significantly reduce the incidence of female-headed families because of the powerful forces at work in our society which are leading to family disintegration. In fact, there is evidence that family dissolution will continue apace when welfare is made available to one- and two-parent families equally.[29] But we must eliminate any tendency of the welfare system to exacerbate this tragedy. Currently only a minority of states even allow two-parent families to participate in AFDC.[30] Federal guidelines should require all states to do so.

A fourth direction for reform would be to encourage tenant ownership of public housing. Personal home ownership brings self-esteem and economic independence. We now subsidize middle- and upper-class private home ownership through a one hundred per cent mortgage-interest tax deduction. If we reduced this tax benefit for the rich (for example, by reducing the percentage of interest that is deductible on homes costing over one hundred thousand dollars), we could find significant resources to promote private home ownership for the poor.

These four reforms, however, will not solve the problem of long-term welfare dependency. Although only a minority of the welfare population is dependent on welfare for long periods, it is not an insignificant portion. A study of AFDC recipients who began receiving benefits in 1970 found that about half remained on welfare for one year, sixteen to eighteen per cent for five years and five to seven per cent for ten years.[31] Another study of AFDC recipients over a seven-year period examined both the length of time spent on welfare and the proportion of total income derived from benefits. Eleven per cent of the recipients were long-term users (over six years), and welfare payments provided over half of their total income.[32] In a different ten-year study, forty per cent of the new AFDC recipients remained on welfare for five years or more. Furthermore, new female recipients usually applied for aid because of the departure of a husband or the birth of a child out of wedlock.[33]

If we are to reduce long-term poverty and dependency, we will have to look beyond the welfare system and address the causes of illegitimacy, separation and divorce, and inadequate job opportunities. Central to a solution of these problems will be personal conversion and the teaching of biblical values about sexual purity and lifelong marriage covenant. Central too is the availability for all of jobs with decent pay so that everyone can support themselves and their families. But we dare not let people starve while we seek vigorously for long-term solutions.

These suggestions on welfare reform do not constitute a comprehensive public-policy agenda for eliminating poverty in the United States. Other government programs that have succeeded in reducing the incidence of poverty should be continued or expanded. Observers from many political persuasions have recognized the success of the Job Corps, Head Start, compensatory education for disadvantaged children, and nutritional aid to women, infants and children. All have real benefits for our future work force.[34] The welfare system is no substitute for a healthy economy, or for equal opportunity for employment and housing, or for investment in the education of all people, especially the disadvantaged. By itself the welfare system will not end poverty. But it is an essential safety net.

Tax Reform

Two-thirds of all taxpayers believe that they have to pay more than their fair share of taxes. At least that is what they said in a poll commissioned by the Internal Revenue Service in 1984. Eighty per cent believe that the system benefits the rich and is unfair to the ordinary working man or woman. According to former I.R.S. Commissioner Roscoe L. Egger, Jr., such feelings threaten the viability of the entire federal tax system. If disenchanted taxpayers cease to comply voluntarily with the tax laws, the government would face an expensive and hopeless task of trying to wrest taxes from unwilling citizens. In 1981, the latest year for which figures are available, it is estimated that U.S. taxpayers failed to pay $90 billion in taxes they owed. One can see why Egger fears we are getting close to a society in which "dodging taxes becomes not only fashionable, but acceptable."[35]

Taxes are necessary if government is to continue to fulfill its role as an instrument of justice. But how should taxes be raised? No tax system is perfect. Tax policy requires difficult choices among frequently competing goals. Experts express these in different ways, but usually include the following three elements.[36]

1. *Taxpayers in the same financial circumstances should pay the same amount of taxes.* This is fundamental to any fair and equitable tax system.

2. *Taxpayers should be taxed according to their ability to pay.* Those with higher incomes or greater wealth should pay more, and those with lower incomes or less wealth should pay less. In tax jargon, a tax is *proportional* if all taxpayers pay the same percentage of their incomes in taxes. It is *progressive* if the percentage rises with

income, and *regressive* if the percentage falls. The biblical teaching that God is opposed to extremes of wealth and poverty would seem to favor progressive taxes on income and wealth. Proportional or regressive taxes merely perpetuate, or even worsen, such extremes. According to a recent study by Brookings Institution economist Joseph Pechman, the total U.S. tax system—including all federal, state and local taxes—is either mildly progressive or slightly regressive, depending on one's assumptions about who ends up paying certain taxes. Under the more progressive assumptions, the poorest tenth of Americans pay 21.9% of their incomes in taxes; the wealthiest tenth of Americans pay an average of 25.3%. By contrast, in 1966 the poorest paid 16.8% and the richest paid 30.1%, respectively.[37] Today the poor pay more and the rich pay less!

3. *The tax system should promote a healthy economy.* Taxes should not hamper economic growth by reducing work, savings and investment. Nor should they arbitrarily distort incentives provided by the market economy. Except when intentionally used to correct problems in the private economy or to pursue other policies in the public interest (for example, providing incentives for energy conservation), the tax system should not influence the direction of economic activity. Therefore, tax laws should not benefit particular industries at the expense of others. Nor should they encourage wasteful investment in tax shelters which produce little or no benefit to the economy. One component of this principle is that taxes should be easily and cheaply collected. Excessive administrative costs to the government and taxpayers are an unnecessary drain on the economy.

To these principles I would add another:

4. *Tax structures should strengthen, not weaken, the family and the lifelong marriage covenant.* The tax system should promote the ability of men and women to join in families, support themselves and care for their members.

Trends in federal tax laws violated all four principles. In the

1970s and early 1980s, taxes for low-income working families rose sharply, while those of the wealthy declined. Tax shelters proliferated. The taxation of corporations became unfair and economically unsound. Estate (that is, inheritance) taxes virtually disappeared.

Many proposals have been made to reform the federal income tax.[38] One would replace it with a consumption tax. Such a tax is based not on annual income, but annual spending (annual income minus net savings). Since poorer people spend a larger portion of their incomes than do richer people, a straight consumption tax would be regressive. Over time, it also would increase concentrations of wealth, since savings could accumulate without being taxed. In theory, corrections could be made, but they would make the tax much more complicated and harder for taxpayers to understand. Moreover, a change to a consumption tax would cause huge disruptions in the economy. A consumption tax is not the way to go.[39]

Another proposal is to use a national sales tax or a value-added tax. (A value-added tax is imposed on the purchaser of a product, whether a business or individual; it is passed along to eventual consumers and has an economic effect much like a sales tax.) Once again, this tax would be regressive, because poorer people spend more of their incomes than do richer folk. Providing low-income relief would once again be administratively complex.[40]

I believe that improvement of the existing income and estate taxes would be more in keeping with the biblical understanding of justice. However structured, it should reduce taxes for poor families, end tax breaks for many corporations and wealthy taxpayers, and restore significant, but not total, taxation of large estates.

As this book was being finished, Congress approved the most significant reform of the federal income tax since it was first adopted in 1913. The Tax Reform Act of 1986 dramatically cuts tax rates for individuals and corporations, and pays for the loss of tax revenue by eliminating or reducing many tax loopholes. It also provides badly needed tax relief for millions of poor Americans and ensures that large, profitable corporations pay substantial taxes.

This bill embodies a number of significant reforms and is indeed an impressive achievement in making a more just tax system. It should not mark the end of efforts at tax reform, however, since other problems remain to be addressed.

Taxes on the Poor

In 1981 Congress approved a twenty-three per cent cut in personal income tax rates over a three-year period. Wealthy taxpayers enjoyed significant tax savings as a result. But poor people, especially poor families, saw their taxes soar! A family of four at the poverty level paid $460 in federal income and Social Security taxes in 1980 and $1,076 in 1984.[41] Is that the way the biblical prophets would write tax laws?

Two developments help explain how this injustice occurred. First, the regressive payroll tax that funds the Social Security system has continued to rise since 1981 and is scheduled to rise even further. In 1985 it took 7.05% of the first $39,000 of every wage- and salary-earner's paycheck. (Employers pay an equivalent amount, but most economists believe that employees end up paying it in the form of lower wages; the effective tax rate is therefore 14.1%.) Persons earning more than $39,000, and those with substantial nonwage income (usually wealthy persons) pay a smaller percentage of their incomes in payroll taxes. For the working poor, on the other hand, their entire income is taxed for Social Security. In fact, the working poor often pay as much in Social Security taxes as they do in income taxes. Therefore, the increase in this tax has had a much more significant impact on the total tax burden of poor working families.[42]

Second, inflation has, until recently, eroded the value of the most important forms of tax relief for poor families: the personal exemption, the standard deduction and the earned income credit (which was passed specifically to relieve the burden of the Social Security tax on low-income families).[43] The new tax law has made significant inroads in reversing this erosion and making the income tax once again progressive at low-income levels.

When fully implemented, the 1986 Tax Reform Act will nearly double the personal exemption to $2,000, substantially raise the standard deductions to $3,000 for single persons and $5,000 for married couples, and boost the maximum earned-income tax credit from $550 to $800. Now about twice as many families (those with incomes up to $17,000) are able to qualify for the earned income credit. As a result of these changes, six million poor Americans will be removed from the income tax rolls. A family of four will not begin to pay any income taxes until its income reaches $13,000; under the old system, that family paid $650 in taxes. In fact, a family of four not only will be taken off the tax rolls in that case, the earned income credit will offset half of their Social Security taxes. The Tax Reform Act will index all three of these provisions to the inflation rate, thus preventing inflation from eroding their value, as occurred in the past.

Yet nothing in this bill would change the regressive Social Security tax, which will continue to rise (in fact, is scheduled to rise in order to keep the Social Security system afloat) and to unfairly burden low- and middle-income wage earners. Although they may not pay any income tax, poor workers will still pay Social Security tax. True, the earned income credit will offset some of this burden, but reform is still in order. The burden of the Social Security tax should be largely, if not entirely, refunded through the income tax credit for the poor. This will increase the incomes of the poor, enhance the rewards of work, and help them to become self-sufficient.

Corporate Taxes
All Western industrial nations levy taxes on corporate profits

The country with the highest corporate taxes is Japan, whose tax code was modeled after that of the United States in the 1950s. Revenues raised from corporate taxes are about 5% of Japan's GNP and account for 28% of total government revenue.[44]

Since the 1950s, the picture in the United States has changed drastically. Federal corporate income tax revenues have fallen from 6.5% of GNP in 1951 to 1.7% in the early 1980s. As a share of total federal revenue, the corporate income tax has fallen from 23.4% in 1960 to 10.2% in 1981.[45] The weight of corporate income taxes is borne by the holders of corporate stock—namely, the most wealthy segment of the population. Consequently, the decline in corporate taxes has decreased the progressivity of federal taxes.[46] Again, the rich win and the poor lose.

In fact, many large, profitable corporations pay no taxes at all. A study of 250 large corporations found that, in at least one of the three years between 1981 and 1983, 128 of them paid no federal income taxes. Some even received rebates! Yet these same 128 companies earned cumulative profits of $57.1 billion. The biggest gainer was General Electric, which earned $6.5 billion in profits over the three years, but received $238 million in tax refunds. Seventeen companies paid zero or less in each of the three years. These included such large defense contractors as GE, Boeing, General Dynamics, Lockheed and Grumman, all of whom profited from the defense build-up of the 1980s but paid nothing toward it.[47] Alas for Isaiah, who thought that the way to peace was justice.

The new tax bill reverses a twenty-year trend by increasing the corporate income tax and addressing some of the injustices mentioned above. Corporate taxes will not be increased by raising tax rates, however. Indeed, the tax rate for all but the smallest corporations will fall from 46% to 34%. The revenue will be raised by eliminating or reducing many tax breaks. Most significant is the repeal of the investment tax credit (a tax that benefited only capital-intensive industries), which by itself will raise $125 billion over five years. The accelerated depreciation deductions possible under the 1981 tax cut will be reduced slightly by extending the write-off periods and delaying some of the deductions to later years. Tax depreciation still does not represent true economic depreciation, and so further reform in this area is needed. The current changes alone raise about $13 billion in tax revenue. A strengthened "minimum tax" provision will ensure that no profitable corporations escape taxation altogether, as they have been doing, and will raise another $31 billion. Many other special corporate tax breaks also will be curtailed, although some will remain. The net effect, however, will be to treat all corporations alike, reducing the tax disparities among industries. The result is a fairer and economically more efficient tax code. Even though corporate taxes will rise, the respected economic consulting firm Data Resources, Inc., predicted that the U.S. economy would grow at a much faster rate than without the tax reform.[48]

The Reform Act will also virtually eliminate many of the tax shelters used by wealthy taxpayers. For example, paper losses in limited-partnership investment schemes could no longer be used to avoid paying taxes on income from salaries or other investments. This provision alone will raise about $20 billion in revenue over five years. The repeal of the capital gains preference also will reduce incentives to funnel money into wasteful tax shelters. Financial decisions would be made on their own merits, not on the basis of their tax implications. And rich taxpayers would no longer pay less in taxes than the working poor. The resentment and cynicism which now threaten our voluntary payment of taxes might be reduced.

Inheritance Taxes
In the previous chapter, we saw how God condemns extremes of wealth and poverty. I have argued that progressive taxes (where the rich pay a higher percentage than do the poor) is one contemporary way to implement this biblical principle. Progressive taxes make it harder for such extremes to develop. But if taxes are

too high, most economists believe they will discourage work, savings and investment. What else might we do?

English economist and Nobel laureate Sir James Meade once compared three different ways of bringing about a more equal distribution of wealth and opportunity in society. Strengthening trade unions, he said, would not work, because unions would push for higher wages and cause inflation. Steeply progressive taxes would hamper economic activity. The only feasible solution that he saw was the broad distribution of property wealth. "Extreme inequalities in the ownership of property are undesirable, quite apart from any inequalities of income which they may imply," he said, because they also mean "an unequal distribution of power."[49] As we have seen, the decentralization of power is a biblical mandate. It also lies at the base of democratic theory and practice. Since money is power, extremes are dangerous. But wealth tends to concentrate in a laissez-faire economy. Meade concluded that we should redistribute property rather than income.

How might wealth be taxed to accomplish such redistribution? A property tax is one obvious way. But such taxes are generally limited to real estate, not stocks, bonds, gold and valuables. Many economists believe that real-estate property taxes are regressive, because nonwealthy people must spend a higher proportion of their incomes on housing.[50] Eight European countries tax more than real estate via an annual wealth tax. But only the very richest are taxed. Many types of property are still exempt, and rates are very low—Sweden has the highest top rate, at 2.5%. Such a tax never has been seriously proposed in the United States and probably would be politically unacceptable.[51]

The inheritance tax, which the United States has used for many years, is another possibility. Meade thought that an important part of wealth redistribution should be a system of inheritance taxation. He argued, and most economists agree, that a tax on inheritances is less destructive of economic incentives than an income tax that raises the same amount of revenue.[52] Moreover, in a society that rightly protects private property, taxation of inheritances is less intrusive than a straight tax on wealth. The state has for centuries regulated the transfer of property to the next generation, and an inheritance tax merely conditions that transfer.[53]

In the United States, the federal government levies a tax on estates—that is, on the privilege of transferring wealth at one's death. Transfers (gifts) are taxed the same way. This prevents the avoidance of estate taxes by transferring property before death.

Tax rates on estates are fairly high, ranging from 18% on the first $10,000 of taxable estate to 50% on amounts over $2.5 million. But nobody who thinks to hire an accountant or lawyer pays anywhere near that much! The estate tax code is full of loopholes and exemptions. In fact, it exempts most estates altogether. In 1985, the first $400,000 of an estate was exempted. In 1986 this rose to $500,000, and in 1987 and thereafter it will be $600,000. By the time the new law is completely in effect, less than one per cent of estates will be taxed.[54]

I believe the United States should tax more estates by lowering these exemptions and eliminating the loopholes. This was not done in the 1986 reform. The rates need not be high, and in fact, might be lower than the current rate schedule. Exemptions should be provided for a family home and necessary items of personal property (such as the family car). Moreover, the current provision which permits a tax-free transfer to the surviving spouse should be continued. Special consideration should also be given to family-owned-and-operated farms and small businesses so that the estate tax does not discourage these smaller family enterprises.[55] But if the estate tax is to be a real agent of avoiding extremes of wealth and poverty, we must close the loopholes and lower the exemptions.

Not all will agree that the proposed changes in welfare policies and tax laws are the best way to implement economic justice.[56] Christians who disagree with these proposals should articulate other policies which they consider better. But if we are Christians and want Christ to be the Lord of our politics, then a central part of the ongoing debate must be the question: What policy revisions in the welfare system and the tax laws will be most likely to implement the biblical summons to empower the poor, discourage extremes of wealth and poverty, move in the direction of equality of economic opportunity and strengthen the family? Only those who are willing to submit their proposals to that test can claim to endorse a consistently biblical pro-life agenda.

Part 3

SEXUALITY, FEMINISM AND THE FAMILY

Chapter 6

The Biblical Promise

"The LORD was witness to the covenant between you and the wife of your youth." *Malachi 2:14*

S ome contemporaries view the family as an outdated, oppressive system that liberated folk must quickly cast aside. Biblical faith portrays the family as a divine gift essential for abundant living. A biblical pro-life agenda would be radically incomplete without a major focus on sexuality and the family.

Western society is sick. Through decades of obstinate rebellion against God's intention, modern folk have lost the joy of sexuality and the security, happiness and fulfillment of the family. Divorce, spouse and child abuse, and sexual perversion run rampant. Agony and hell haunt our homes.

God intended something far different. Biblical faith offers the promise of hope. Even today, following God's intention for sexuality and for the family will still lead to joy and fulfillment.

What is the shape of this biblical promise? And how might government provide modest support for the realization of this promise?

Created for Mutual Interdependence

God created humanity in a way that genuine fulfillment is possible only in mutual interdependence between man and woman. Autonomous individualism and unisexual ideals are not the intention of the One who created woman and man in the divine image. Our existence as deeply different yet genuinely equal sexes who reach fulfillment only in mutual relationship is central to the divine plan: "So God created man in his own image, in the image of God he created him; male and female he created them" (Gen 1:27). An uncle's gentle teasing of a favorite niece, an exhilarating debate between male and female faculty colleagues, and a warm Christian embrace between sister and brother in the public assembly of believers all reflect the joyful goodness of human sexuality that God intended when he created us male and female.

Marriage is the divinely willed context for the deepest relationship of mutual interdependence between man and woman. Marriage is not a human invention. As Jesus clearly taught, it is a divine institution embedded in the very structure of the created order:

From the very beginning of creation, "God made them male and female. For this reason a man shall leave his father and mother and be joined to his wife, and the two shall become one flesh." So they are no longer two but one flesh. What therefore God has joined together, let not man put asunder. (Mk 10:6-9)[1]

One important place where contemporary loneliness and alienation find their solution is in the Creator's merciful gift of mutually interdependent spouses.

Nothing underlines the goodness of marriage more powerfully than the fact that the Bible repeatedly uses language about marriage in a symbolic way to describe the loving relationship between God and his people. The Old Testament frequently calls Israel God's wife (Is 50:1; 54:4-6) or bride (Jer 2:2; Hos 2:10-20). Jesus is the bridegroom (Mk 2:19-20) eagerly awaited by the church, his pure bride (2 Cor 11:2).[2]

To say that marriage is embedded in creation itself is not to make it an ultimate good in life. That honor belongs only to God and God's kingdom. Our relationship to God matters more than marriage or family (Mt 10:34-38; 19:29). All those who enter the kingdom are part of Jesus' new family (Mt 12:46-48). Singleness too is a divine gift that can be offered in joyful fulfillment and mutual interdependence to others in church and society. In those cases, the goodness of human sexual difference is enjoyed in the purity of sexual abstinence in intimate male-female relationships in the family and the church. But to say with Jesus that marriage is rooted in creation is to assert that it is the normal context for experiencing intimate male-female relations.

Tragically, modern folk have sought liberation in autonomous individuality. Radical feminism has encouraged women to catch up with men in that rebellious revolt which places self-fulfillment above family obligation. Many husbands have long placed greater priority on business success or extramarital sex than on family obligations. Many wives now match men's tragic selfishness as they rank personal self-fulfillment above commitment to husband and children. Sociologists Brigette and Peter Berger put it well: "The family, at best, is reduced to being one of many freely chosen and freely disposable mechanisms whose purpose is the fostering of the individual's project of self-attainment."[3] Lifelong marriage cannot survive such seductive silliness. To realize the full promise of marriage, covenant loyalty must outrank individual self-realization. Paradoxically, self-denial is the path to self-fulfillment.

Called to a Lifelong Covenant

Jesus' teaching is unambiguous. God's will for marriage is a man and a woman committed in holy covenant for life. So sacred is marriage that the Creator of the galaxies stoops to serve as witness: "The Lord was witness to the covenant between you and the wife of your youth, to whom you have been faithless, though she is your companion and your wife by covenant" (Mal 2:14). No one dare tear asunder the covenant of lifelong loyalty made in the presence of the divine Covenant Partner.

The Scriptures repeatedly summon spouses to the same kind of steadfast loyalty God has revealed in his covenant with us. The Hebrew word *hesed* refers to God's covenant loyalty. The word *hesed* is so rich that it is translated with several words: "loving kindness," "steadfast love," "mercy." It is that covenant loyalty that moved God to continue loving his sinful people in spite of persistent disobedience. It is that covenant loyalty described by Hosea when he proclaims to Israel that after God punishes her disobedience God will betroth her to himself forever: "I will betroth you to me for ever; I will betroth you to me in righteousness and in justice, and in steadfast love *[hesed]*, and in mercy" (Hos 2:19; see also Lam 3:22-23). It is the kind of covenant loyalty Hosea offered to his adulterous wife (Hos 1—3).

Hesed is the kind of self-sacrificing loyalty to which Ephesians 5 summons husbands (and wives): "Husbands, love your wives, as Christ loved the church, and gave himself up for her" (5:25). Christ's love for us goes on and on. It goes all the way to the cross. The Bible calls spouses to imitate this divine, persistent, sacrificial covenant loyalty.

That is not to say lifelong covenant is easy. It involves painful forgiving and steadfast faithfulness. Sometimes disobedience compounds wrong choices and divorce results. Even then the divine Covenant Partner forgives those who repent. But divorce is never God's will (Mal 2:15-16; Mk 10:6-9; 1 Cor 7:10-11). The Old Testament, to be sure, permitted it because of the hardness of sinful hearts (Deut 24:1; Mk 10:5). But Jesus taught that from creation, lifelong covenant loyalty was the divine intention (Mk 10:6-9). And since Christ came to restore wholeness to a fallen creation, he, therefore, calls his disciples to live now as members of the restored creation.

To a promiscuous, self-seeking society misled by false dreams

of autonomous individualism, the idea of exclusive, lifelong covenant loyalty seems both confining and impossible. But it is, finally, the only way to genuine fulfillment and freedom in marriage.

It is the mystery of love in marriage that commitment leads to
freedom—freedom to move out from a sure base of security
and acceptance, freedom to plumb all my creativity, freedom to
be my authentic self much more than if I did not have such
security. Jesus told us in his teaching, "Whoever would save his
life will lose it; and whoever loses his life for my sake, he will
save it" (Luke 9:24 and pars.). The truth of that teaching becomes abundantly clear in the relationship of marriage. When
we commit ourselves, when we give ourselves to each other in
the relation of matrimony, when we lose ourselves in a total
and accepting dedication to the other, then we most surely find
our freedom to be ourselves, then we most fully discover that
we can live and love.[4]

Invited to the Joy of Committed Sex

The Bible exults in the joy of sex. Nowhere is the biblical affirmation of the goodness of the material world more clear than in
the description of Adam and Eve as naked and unashamed (Gen
2:24-25) and in the Song of Solomon's sensuous, erotic poetry.
Misled by Augustinian asceticism and Victorian prudery, some
Christians may still blush at biblical frankness. But not the Creator.

God intended sex between committed spouses to involve mutual
ecstasy and passionate joy. The mutuality of love is especially vivid
in the Song of Solomon. Richard Foster comments,

Nowhere in the book do you find the dull story of man acting
and the woman being acted upon—quite the contrary! Both are
intensely involved; both initiate; both receive. It is as if the
curse of man's domination that resulted from the Fall has been
surmounted by the grace of God. Even the literary structure of
the book emphasizes that love is reciprocal. The man speaks;

the woman speaks; the chorus sings the refrain. . . . Both are constantly giving and receiving in the act of love, love's mutuality.[5]

That kind of joy is most likely to be experienced and sustained within the committed relationship of lifelong covenant. The right context for sex is between a man and woman who have covenanted together before the divine Witness to be faithful to each other for better or worse, till death do them part. Adultery is wrong (Ex 20:14; Mt 5:27-30).[6] Premarital sex is wrong (Ex 22:16-17, Mt 15:19).[7] Only within lifelong covenant, can human sex realize its full promise.

Autonomous secular humanists scorn such limitations. Freedom to them means no restrictions on individual choices. Extramarital affairs, open marriage, free communal sex and homosexual, lesbian or bisexual relationships are all good, they claim, if the individual finds them self-fulfilling. To be sure, any honest Christian faithfully married for 25 or 40 years will never deny that the temporary excitement of hot passion in extramarital sex has appeal. Sexual love in a lifelong marriage is, in Richard Foster's fine phrase, a mixture of "tenderness and halitosis, love and fatigue, ecstasy and disappointment."[8]

But the Christian also knows that it is only in a committed marriage that sex reaches its deepest promise. If the relationship depends on constant performance, even the performance flounders. The popular songwriters know that "true love is forever." The physical intimacy and total self-disclosure of sex cry out for an exclusive lasting commitment. Only in the radical security of the knowledge that temporary failure will not threaten one's partner's commitment can sex truly blossom.

From the biblical perspective, the purpose of sex is both procreation of the race and the joy of marital intimacy and unity. The responsibility and privilege to pass on the gift of life to the next generation needs to be emphasized in our age of self-seeking and anxiety. It is through the intimacy of sex that God chooses to populate the earth with persons created in the divine image. And it is in the security of a lifelong marriage covenant that God wills children to develop into responsible adults.

Equally important is the unitive function of sex clearly stated both in Genesis and by Jesus. It is in intercourse that married partners become fully "one flesh" (Gen 2:25; Mk 10:8-9). So important is this joy of sexual union that Deuteronomy 24:5 stipulates that the newly married should be free of military and business responsibilities for a full year to enjoy each other. The Scriptures underline this unitive function of marital sex by using the verb "to know" to describe intercourse (Gen 4:1; 1 Sam 1:19-20). "Sex is to be a 'knowing,' a way of intimacy that can be realized in no other way."[9]

At its best, sexual intercourse is a kind of flowing together: an overwhelming hunger and drive to join bodies as one, a feverish working together for realization, ecstasy so great it is almost painful, and then release, deep contentment and security and happiness in the arms of each other. In the process of sexual intercourse, we feel as if the most hidden inner depths of our beings are brought to the surface and revealed and offered to each other as the most intimate expression of our love. All we are as male or female become open to the other, and is made complete by being joined with the inner self of one's mate. We know each other and become one with the other and are fulfilled by each other in a way otherwise utterly impossible, and that knowing and that fulfillment carry over into our whole married life, and strengthen and deepen and periodically refresh it.[10]

Sex Out of Context

Sex is a wonderful gift from God.

Unfortunately, any contemporary discussion of sex must include not only the Christian ideal, but problem areas such as homosexuality and pornography.

What about gay liberation? Obviously, the one-night stands and disease-filled promiscuity of much contemporary homosexuality and lesbianism are totally wrong. But what about a committed gay relationship? Or a gay marriage?

Christians certainly must repent of their homophobic past.[11] Homosexual sin is no worse than adulterous sin. Furthermore, we must distinguish clearly between homosexual orientation and homosexual practice. Homosexual orientation is not sinful just as heterosexual desire for sex outside marriage is not sinful—unless one lingers over and seeks to implement these fantasies. Christians need to love, support and welcome in the church people who acknowledge a homosexual orientation and who call on God and God's people to help them live a life of abstinence. We must also weep and pray with those who fail and repent.

Condoning homosexual practice, however, is entirely different. If our norm is biblical revelation rather than current fashion, then Christians will insist that homosexual practice is contrary to God's will.

The biblical case against practicing homosexuality does not rest primarily on the few explicit words of condemnation (although those are present and clear). It rests primarily on the constant, pervasive biblical teaching that sex is a gift intended only for the committed relationship of a man and a woman in lifelong covenant. Never is there a hint anywhere in Scripture that God intended sex in any other relationship.

But the explicit prohibitions are also there—and clear, in spite of the special pleading of some recent pro-gay exegesis.[12] The Old Testament condemns it (Lev 18:22; 20:13). Paul lists homosexuality in a long catalog of sins that prevent people from inheriting the kingdom of God (1 Cor 6:9-10; 1 Tim 1:8-10).[13] Romans 1:26-27 is especially clear:

> Their women exchanged natural relations for unnatural, and the men likewise gave up natural relations with women and were consumed with passion for one another, men committing

shameless acts with men and receiving in their own persons the due penalty for their error.

It requires considerable exegetical gymnastics to argue plausibly that this passage does not exclude all homosexual practice.[14]

Pornography is also a terrible distortion of God's good gift of sex. Pornography abuses little children, women and men. It corrupts societal moral standards and probably encourages sexual crimes.[15] We must find ways to limit its demonic impact on our children and our total society. The Attorney General's Commission on Pornography (July 1986) has supplied the ghastly data and pointed toward a solution. Basically, they recommend that the laws already on the books be enforced—vigorously. Citizens—including millions of Christian citizens—must demand action now.[16]

There is a way to correct the agony and hell of today's sexual wilderness. It is to return to the limits God provided when he gave us this wonderful gift.

The Role of Parents in the Family

The Bible places awesome responsibility on parents. It also gives them the authority to meet those obligations.

The fundamental responsibility for rearing children rests with parents, not the state. Parents are to provide for far more than the physical needs of their children. They are to be their children's primary teachers in morality and faith. Whereas recent thought (illustrated, for instance, by the Carnegie Council on the Family) has despaired of parents as the major source of training in moral values, the Bible insists on this crucial role.[17] Parents are to teach God's law to their children "when you sit in your house, and when you walk by the way, and when you lie down, and when you rise" (Deut 6:6-7). Indeed, so important is this teaching role that fathers who fail to nurture disciplined, devout children are said to be unworthy of leadership in the church (1 Tim 3:4-5; Tit 1:6).

From the fifth commandment to the epistles of Paul, the Scriptures insist that children honor and obey their parents (Ex 20:12; Col 3:20; Eph 6:1-2). The Bible knows nothing of the modern liberal notion that children should have equal or near equal authority in the family. Without being authoritarian or harsh (Col 3:21; Eph 6:4), parents may discipline their children and demand obedience because they possess divinely given authority in the home.

Too many modern parents—first fathers and then mothers—have placed financial success, careers or even personal fulfillment above their responsibilities as parents. Fathers, and now mothers, increasingly fail to spend the time at home needed to provide the love, security, stability and training that children need. The self-centeredness which leads to divorce is perhaps the most blatant way this happens. But it also occurs when professional careers or desire for greater affluence seduce both parents of young children to work full time outside the home. In 1972, 30% of American women with children under six worked outside the home. In 1982, this had jumped to 49%.[18]

It is time for Christians to defy and denounce this rapidly growing trend. When children are young, one parent should be in the home full-time. It may be the father or the mother or both if each work half-time and stay home half-time.[19] In a time when both women and men rightly have professional careers, this will call for carefully processed and sometimes costly mutual submission. But for most Western parents, who live in the richest societies on earth, to suppose that both *must* work for financial reasons is obscene materialism of the highest order. It is also blatant defiance of the biblical priority of parenting.

It is also essential for Christians to model alternatives to the growing abandonment of parental responsibility through divorce. According to a recent cover story in *Newsweek*, one-half of all American families may be headed by only one adult by 1990.[20] Contemporary social analysis shows the tragic consequences for children who lack the primary role models of both mother and father. Sociologists Brigette and Peter Berger point out that studies clearly demonstrate that children growing up in two-parent homes "have fewer emotional and behavioral problems, do better in school, have higher rates of achievement, and move more easily from dependence to autonomy."[21]

A Social Foundation for Family Life

Many complex factors have contributed to the troubles of the contemporary family. Relativistic moral values, extreme feminism[22] and male authoritarianism have played a significant role. So has the mobility of urban, industrialized society. Specialization and mobility destroy traditional communities, where the nearness of relatives and friends used to strengthen marriages. Nor dare we overlook the importance of economic factors. As the studies on increased alcoholism and family violence demonstrate, unemployment devastates families. Public policy—via welfare programs that penalize the presence of the father and tax codes that make cohabitation financially preferable to marriage—has also added its negative contribution.

It is striking to compare the current scene with family life in ancient Israel.[23] Instead of weakening the family, religious values and socio-economic structures combined together to make the family the central social institution of Israelite life. Religious sanction of parental authority and the sanctity of marriage provided moral strength. The central role of the extended family with its important educational, judicial and welfare functions provided social support. And the laws on land tenure provided a secure economic foundation for self-sufficient families independent of the state.

The Israelite family was larger than the modern nuclear family composed of husband, wife and children (although that nuclear cluster was present). This nuclear cluster with its own house existed within a larger, three- or four-generation extended family. This extended family educated its children. A significant amount of judicial authority rested with the head of the family.[24] And a major part of the welfare arrangements to protect the poor were the responsibility of the larger extended family.[25] For example, close kin of folk who lost their land were to help their impoverished relatives recover it (Lev 25:25).

Financial independence based on ownership of land was the solid economic foundation of the family. The texts suggest that the land had been divided more or less equally among the tribes (Num 33:52-56; Josh 17:14). Presumably, the same equality occurred as each extended family received its land. Right at the heart of the land-tenure laws of the Old Testament is the concern to protect each family's ancestral land.[26] Even if some folk lost their land because of mismanagement, laziness or disability, every fifty years the land was to return to the original families. God wanted each family to have the economic means to earn its own way. Naboth's refusal to sell his ancestral vineyard (1 Kings 21:3) and the frequent prophetic denunciation of the rich and powerful who managed through bribery or violence to seize the land of the poor (for example, Mic 2:2; Is 5:8) both illustrate how central was family ownership of its own land in ancient Israel.

Israelite life differed radically from surrounding Canaanite city-states.[27] There, a king owned all the land and society was highly stratified. Decentralized land ownership by extended families in Israel was crucial for the viability of the basically egalitarian family and their independence from the state. Norman Gottwald summarizes his study of early Israelite society: "[It was] an egalitarian, extended family, segmentary tribal society with an agricultural-pastoral economic base . . . characterized by profound resistance and opposition to the forms of political domination and social stratification that had become normative in the chief cultural and political centers of the ancient Near East."[28]

Feminism and the Family
Is feminism destroying the family? Extreme feminism certainly is.

There are a small number of extreme feminists who describe heterosexuality as rape, motherhood as slavery, and all relations between men and women as a power struggle. The traditional family is the enemy. The solution is lesbianism, industrialization of housework, and public care of children from birth.[29] These extreme feminist ideas are unbiblical and destructive.

But is there a biblical feminism that strengthens rather than weakens the family?

That men have oppressed women is painfully clear. Historically, men have too often viewed women as inferior beings of weaker intellect whose major value was that of cook, housekeeper and sex object. Women had to fight for the vote. They faced major discrimination as they tried to enter the professions. And they still receive lower pay than men for comparable work. (See table 1.[30])

Is there any biblical support for these feminist concerns? Women were certainly not viewed as the equals of men in patriarchal Israel. But Genesis and Jesus offer an astonishing picture of the dignity of women.

Genesis 1:26-28 teaches that the dominion over the earth given to humanity is a dominion given to both male and female. Both are created in the image of God. It is only with the Fall that the Bible introduces any notion of male domination over women. Because of their sinful rebellion God punishes the guilty pair. Part of Eve's punishment is that her husband will "rule over" her (Gen 3:16).

Elizabeth Achtemeier makes the point powerfully:

Here, in profoundest terms, is where the battle of the sexes begins: in our flight from God and our prideful attempts to be our own masters. The role of man over woman is finally the result of sin. . . . Just how the author of Genesis, Chapter 3, could have laid hold of such a view in the ancient Near Eastern world in the tenth century B.C. seems beyond rational explanation. He must have been grasped by the most radical revelation of God's desire for his universe. Such a view flew in the

Table 1. Median Earnings in 1982 for Full-Time Workers, by Race

OCCUPATION	WHITE		BLACK		HISPANICS	
	Women	Men	Women	Men	Women	Men
Executives, Administrators & Managerial	$17,518	$30,388	$17,403	$21,008	$16,761	$22,673
Professional Specialty Occupations	18,307	27,712	16,747	20,265	15,187	27,392
Technicians and Related	15,399	22,472	14,814	14,502	13,589	19,285
Sales	11,253	22,819	10,466	15,318	9,963	17,640
Administrative Support	12,920	20,870	12,814	17,226	12,384	14,776
Service	9,080	15,169	9,523	12,500	8,350	11,942
Craftsmen and Repairers	13,960	21,807	15,793	17,033	11,448	16,918
Operations and Laborers	10,955	17,665	11,305	15,041	8,969	14,154
Farming, Forestry, Fishing	7,764	12,102	8,245	8,129	6,466	10,813
TOTAL	$13,520	$22,149	$12,355	$15,596	$11,261	$15,446

face of the customs and beliefs of every civilization of the ancient world, and still today it represents a totally unique position.[31]

It is a perspective, however, confirmed by the life and ministry of Jesus. Coming to restore fallen creation to its intended wholeness, Jesus cut through centuries of male discrimination and treated women as equals.

According to Jews of the time, a woman's word had no authority in court.[32] It was a disgrace for men to appear publicly with women. A widely used prayer recommended for daily use by Jewish males thanked God that they had not been created a Gentile, an ignorant man or a woman![33] Jesus, on the other hand appeared publicly with women (Jn 4:27), taught them theology (Lk 10:38- 42) and honored them with his first resurrection appearance.

Messianic prophecy had predicted that in the last days sons and daughters, men and women would prophesy (Joel 2:28; Acts 2:17-18). In the early church that prophecy came true. Women prophesied (Acts 21:9; 1 Cor 11:5) and corrected the theology of men (Acts 18:24-26). Liberated from the restrictions of the synagogue, women participated eagerly in early Christian services.[34] So transformed were male-female relationships that Paul could exclaim: "There is neither Jew nor Greek, there is neither slave nor free, there is neither male nor female; for you are all one in Christ Jesus" (Gal 3:28).

The fundamental equality of the sexes in Jesus' new community did not mean that all differences were denied. Equality does not mean identity. Paul taught that the husband is the head of the wife. But it is a headship immersed in mutual submission and sacrificial servanthood. In Ephesians 5 the instructions for husbands and wives begin with a call for mutual submission: "Be subject to one another" (v. 21). Husbands are to give themselves in loving service to their wives in the same radical way that Christ gave himself for the church (vv. 25-28). What a revolutionary suggestion in the male-chauvinist world of the first century!

Elizabeth Achtemeier sums up this astonishing passage:

The passage is ingenious. It has preserved the traditional view of the male as the head of the family, but that headship is a function only, not a matter of status or superiority. The understanding of the headship and of the wife's relation to it has been radically transformed. There is no lording it over the other here, no exercise of sinful power, no room for unconcern or hostility toward the other. Instead there is only the full devotion of love, poured out for the other, in imitation of Christ's faithfulness and yearning and sacrifice for his church, and of the church's like response to him. . . . Contrary to the views of many of the feminists, we should have no difficulty in saying yes to this passage as the most perfect pattern for Christian marriage. Who can improve on the love of Christ for us?[35]

Yes, there is a biblical feminism. It affirms that women are equal with men. It affirms that God wants women and men to realize their full potential, develop all their gifts, and provide leadership in church and society without discrimination. And it is a feminism that insists that for both fathers and mothers, the family is a divine institution whose responsibilities and delights far outweigh economic status, professional career or short-term self-fulfillment.

Chapter 7

The Family and Public Policy

Census data suggests single-parent families are growing at twenty times the rate of two-parent families.[1]
Armand Nicholi, Harvard University

From the biblical perspective it is the height of absurdity to look to the state to save the family. That is not to deny an important role for public policy. But it is to insist that the crucial battles lie elsewhere.

The survival of the family in the West largely depends on whether Christians and Jews have the integrity to live the moral values they claim and believe. Will we reject Hollywood's sexual nonsense? Will we place family ahead of affluence, promotion and career? The real battle over the family will be won or lost congregation by congregation, preacher by preacher, family by family, individual by individual. It is essentially a battle of moral and religious values. Larger sociological and cultural trends, of course, do influence us all profoundly. Therefore we must also reshape public policy (both nongovernmental and governmental).

Nongovernment Public Institutions
A conscious decision to shape the arts and media (film, television, radio, books and popular music) is necessary. If the only excellent

scripts examined by that small elite that controls our television and film always portray broken homes, sexual perversity, petty parents and rebellious children, then we need to expand that tiny circle. We need sophisticated, carefully researched campaigns, even wisely chosen economic boycotts.

Christians who work in family "helping professions" need firmly to oppose peers whose "scientific" or tolerant approach to family problems denigrate biblical values. And they need to show, using the language and methods of their profession, the benefits to society of healthy families.

Christians also should challenge employers, unions and professional associations to take into account the needs of families when establishing employment policies. The demands of the modern specialized economy, buttressed by rigid attitudes and customs which downplay commitments outside the workplace, make it difficult for a worker to balance the needs of job and home.[2] For example, increased family mobility has weakened traditional neighborhoods with close extended families. That mobility could not be halted without great economic cost or serious infringement of personal freedom. But it would be both desirable and possible for employers and employees to decide to avoid frequent, long-distance moves as much as possible. Society reaps the benefits of the extended family, which is strengthened when parents and children live near grandparents and other close relatives. Businesses, schools and churches should value stronger extended families over the short-term advantages of frequent dislocations of families.

Different policies could also enable workers to arrange employment duties around family responsibilities, rather than the other way around. Helpful too would be expanded opportunities for part-time work, job sharing between two parents, flex-time work schedules, and paid maternity and paternity leaves. We can create responsible, caring employment practices without government coercion. But it will never happen without a concerted effort to educate individuals and corporations. Christians should be at the forefront of this effort.

Government Policy

The focus of this chapter, however, is government policy. We saw that early Israelite values and institutions supported the family morally, socially and economically. How might the state do that today?

A fundamental choice lies at the very beginning. Some propose to save the family by asking the state to perform functions previously handled by the family. It is alleged that the family can no longer handle education, child care, or care of the sick, handicapped and elderly. Instead, agencies funded and controlled by the state must take over these tasks.[3] The alternative is to strengthen the family morally, socially and economically so that a stronger family can handle these problems itself.[4]

If the discussion of biblical values in the previous chapter is correct, then the latter route is the way to go. Furthermore, as we shall see in this chapter, the biblical teaching on the importance of healthy families is confirmed by modern study of child development and accords with the values of democratic process and limited government. This is not to say that government has no role or that we leave all problems to individuals and volunteer agencies. The state has a crucial role, but it must be one that works to strengthen families while keeping them free from government control. Public policy should be concerned primarily with a family's ability to care for its own members, not with displacing the family as an agent of such care.[5]

Family autonomy is essential to the psychological health of children. Goldstein, Freud and Solnit in their well-known book, *Beyond the Best Interests of the Child* insist that "continuity of relationships, surroundings, and environmental influence are essential for a child's normal development."[6] Over time, the constant psychological support and emotional involvement provided by the family turns a helpless child into a self-reliant adult.

These complex and vital developments require the privacy of family life under guardianship by parents who are autonomous. The younger the child, the greater is his need for them. When family integrity is broken or weakened by state intrusion, his needs are thwarted and his belief that his parents are omniscient and all-powerful is shaken prematurely. The effect on the child's developmental progress is invariably detrimental. The child's need for safety within the confines of the family must be met by law through its recognition of family privacy as the barrier to state intrusion upon parental autonomy in child rearing. These rights—parental autonomy, a child's entitlement to autonomous parents, and privacy—are essential ingredients of "family integrity."[7]

These findings call into question the supposed wisdom of relying on the "therapeutic state," whose agencies are allegedly better able to perform many family functions than is the family itself. The state is simply unqualified and unable to supervise the complexities of the parent-child relationship. Its impersonal institutions cannot provide the stable and intense emotional involvement and support needed for a child's healthy development. "The state is too crude an instrument to become an adequate substitute for flesh and blood parents."[8] Therefore, parents should be free to raise their children as they think best with a minimum of state interference.

The raising of children within families has a larger meaning in a democratic society. "Our political system is superimposed on and presupposes a social system of family units, not just of isolated individuals."[9] This is important for two reasons. First, the family is the pre-eminent social institution for inculcating the values and beliefs on which a functioning democracy depends. This includes obedience to legitimate authority and a sense of duty and responsibility toward others. It has been said that "only with a public-spirited, self-sacrificing people could the authority of a popularly elected ruler be obeyed, but 'more by the virtue of the people than by the terror of his power. ' "[10] Such virtue cannot be coerced by the state; it must be taught. And the best place to teach it is in the family.

Psychologists tell us that as children experience the mixture of devotion and discipline uniquely provided by their parents, they best learn to respect authority, to moderate selfishness, and to care for others. Historian Christopher Lasch writes:

> The best argument for the indispensability of the family [is] that children grow up under conditions of "intense emotional involvement" [with their parents]. Without struggling with the ambivalent emotions aroused by the union of love and discipline in his parents, the child never masters his inner rage or his fear of authority. It is for this reason that children need parents, not professional nurses and counselors.[11]

Through this socialization process, a child is able "to internalize moral standards in the form of a conscience."[12] Denied this experience, a child does not grow up. "Psychologically he remains in important ways a child, surrounded by authorities with whom he does not identify and whose authority he does not regard as legitimate."[13]

The second important political reason for maintaining autonomous families is to preserve limited government and prevent state indoctrination and standardization of its citizens. Families provide for many of the health, educational and economic needs of their members. If they did not, most would go unmet or be left to the state. In fact, the state has assumed important functions once performed by families, including education of children and economic security for the aged. But families still fill an important role in limiting the need for bigger government.

If children were raised in state nurseries, the state would have the "capacity to influence powerfully, through socialization, the future outcomes of democratic processes."[14] That citizens "would remain legally free to believe and speak as they wished would not diminish the immense impact of centralizing the processes through which values and beliefs are instilled in the people who will later participate in group decision making."[15] Preserving the family thus preserves diversity, pluralism, religious freedom and democracy.

Courts have given legal force to these principles by reading the Constitution to limit the power of the state to interfere with family life. To a large extent, the family exists, according to a 1944 ruling, as a "private realm of . . . life which the state cannot enter."[16] The courts have insisted that the state cannot prohibit interracial marriage, regulate the choice of birth control or limit which members of one's extended family will live under the same roof.[17] In a number of important cases the Supreme Court has recognized the primacy of the rights of parents in raising and educating their children.[18] Without a compelling governmental interest, such as the protection of the health and safety of a child, the state cannot interfere with parental authority over children. This remains the general rule, even though some exceptions have been made in the name of the rights of children (see pp. 142-44).

In addition to constitutional limits on state power to affect family life, there are very practical limits as well. Public policy can do little to affect such important but intangible elements of family relationships as love, commitment and trust. If husbands and wives cannot bring themselves to live together amicably, or parents will not take an interest in the education of their children, or adolescents will not seek their parents' counsel or respect their wishes, the state has minimal power to make them do so. The law also has a limited ability to enforce moral behavior.

For these religious, constitutional and practical reasons, we must adopt a modest view of government policy regarding the family. Society must tolerate some diversity of values and practices in family life. Not all sins—by whatever definition—should be made crimes.

Yet we should not overlook the pedagogic effect of our laws. In the long term, public laws influence public attitudes toward moral issues, whether for good or ill. If an action is legal, many people assume it is moral as well. Public policy governing the family conveys an important moral message to everyone.

In evaluating the wisdom of a proposed governmental policy initiative affecting the family, we must assess whether the problem is amenable to state control, what pedagogic value the policy serves, and what intrusions into privacy it will entail.

Marriage

For centuries the state has closely regulated the formation and dissolution of marriages. By regulating marital status and clearly designating who is married and who is not, the state controls which relationships enjoy the legal benefits of marriage. These benefits are significant: tax advantages, marital property laws, inheritance rights when no will is in effect, pension benefits, privileged communications between a husband and wife (which the state cannot compel them to disclose), and the right to sue others for the wrongful death or loss of conjugal fellowship and sexual relations with one's spouse.[19]

Some people contend that two persons in a committed relationship, whether or not they are legally married, should enjoy an equal footing with married couples in the eyes of law and public policy. I disagree. This would create an immediate problem of definition. What level of commitment makes a relationship the equivalent of marriage? More significantly, the importance of marriage as a social institution demands that public policy reinforce and strengthen marriage. If we remove all distinction between the married and unmarried in our law and public policy, we will also lose any hope that those instruments can encourage that socially useful behavior on which we now bestow favor and which we call marriage.

If society is to maximize the advantages of healthy family life, the state must provide some minimum parameters for marriage.

Public policy can do this in a positive way by encouraging marriages that are likely to further those societal goals and by supporting the stability of all marital unions. Negatively, it can do this by denying the legal status of "married" (with its attendant benefits) to some categories of relationships.

It is for this reason that children are not, and should not be, permitted to marry. Few of them are mature enough, and few of those unions would be stable enough to further the social values of marriage. Minimum age requirements prevent these marriages which, as experience shows, are likely to break up. Requiring parental consent or premarital counseling for teen-agers who wish to marry accomplishes much the same thing.[20]

More generally, the state regularizes all marriages by requiring a state license, a waiting period and a formal ceremony administered by a party authorized by the state. Although marriage is a civil contract between two persons, unlike most contracts it requires the assent of the state to become effective. This is as it should be. These legal formalities signal the seriousness which the state attaches to marriage. They give the prospective parties time to reconsider what they are doing, and thereby play a modest role in discouraging hasty or ill-considered marriages.[21] The social importance of marriage justifies these minimal intrusions on personal liberty.

It is also important that public policy not directly concerned with marriage not have the side effect of discouraging marriage or encouraging the breakup of marriages. For example, tax and welfare laws at the very minimum should not make two people worse off economically because they decide to get married. Nor should they encourage one parent to leave the family.

How Should We Define the Family?
The definition of the family recognized by law and supported by government policy should be confined, as it has been historically, to groups of people bound by blood, kinship and heterosexual

marriage. Until recently, church, state, and media and family professionals agreed that the ideal family was a mother and father plus their children (perhaps with grandparents or other relatives) living together in their own home. This traditional legal definition obviously includes one-parent households, childless married couples and remarried couples with children from other marriages. But some people today want to extend the definition of family to include unmarried persons who live together, singles households, open marriages, and gay families.[22]

Because these informal relationships are contrary to the Creator's intention, they will not serve the social purposes that the family does, and therefore the state should not accord them equal status.[23] Stable relationships are essential to child development. These are best realized within the commitments provided by formal heterosexual marriages, blood relationships and legal adoption:

> Not all formal families are stable, nor do all necessarily provide wholesome continuity for their children, as the prevailing levels of child abuse and divorce amply demonstrate. But the commitments inherent in formal families do increase the likelihood of stability and continuity for children.[24]

Unmarried cohabitation by definition lacks the same formal, publicly stated and legally binding commitment to permanence that marriage requires. Those who are unwilling to enter into permanent relationships should be denied the legal status of marriage.

Nor do these informal relationships adequately fulfill the political functions of the family. Because their patterns of authority and love are less secure, they are unlikely to do as good a job inculcating needed civic virtues. And they are more likely to invite government intervention and control (to settle child-custody disputes, provide adoption or foster care for children, demand state-run day care and schools to serve child-rearing functions better provided at home). "Impermanent relationships that perform some intimate or associational 'functions' cannot claim the same position as marriage and kinship in ensuring a political structure that limits government, stabilizes social patterns, and protects pluralistic liberty through the power of its own relational permanency."[25]

Broader definitions of marriage and the family also send a troublesome moral lesson to the public. It is therefore important that public policy and law avoid a semantic shift like that which occurred in preparation for the 1980 White House Conference on the Family. Under pressure by advocates of alternative lifestyles and others, it became the White House Conference on Families.[26] We must resist governmental endorsement of moral relativism.

This is not to say that there should be criminal laws against adultery, fornication or homosexual practices between consenting adults conducted in private. Even where such laws still exist, they are seldom enforced. I doubt that they could be enforced against very many offenders. In a pluralistic society where privacy is respected and government is limited, people should be free to make many foolish choices, as long as they do not harm nonconsenting third parties. Furthermore, vigorous enforcement of criminal laws against adultery, fornication or private homosexual practice would involve more government surveillance of and intrusion into private lives than is consistent with our cherished values of individual liberty and privacy.[27]

Civil rights for homosexual sinners should be as secure as civil rights for adulterous sinners, and with few exceptions should be coextensive with the rights of all other sinners. Neither group should be starved or deprived of jobs, housing or the vote, although there may be carefully defined specific jobs—as a schoolteacher or counselor, for instance—from which either or both might rightly be excluded. But government need not and should not allow itself to be used in campaigns to legitimize such practices. Its policy should work with the assumption that these practices are not in the best interests of society and are not one of several equally valid moral options. To do this, government should continue to regulate marriage and maintain the historic legal definitions of marriage and family.

Divorce

What is true of adultery is also true of divorce. The law should not prohibit it, but neither should the law encourage it. Nor should it place divorce and remarriage on a moral par with lifelong marital covenant.

Until recently, state laws made it difficult for couples to divorce. A divorce would be granted to a party only if he or she was able to prove that his or her spouse had committed certain acts which state law deemed sufficient grounds for divorce. These usually included adultery, cruelty and desertion (and in some states, conviction of serious crimes, habitual drunkenness and nonsupport or neglect). A few states allowed divorce based on the parties living apart for a period of time without regard to fault.[28]

The trend in the last twenty years has been to grant divorces more freely. This was done at first by a liberal—sometimes strained—reading of the fault-based grounds for divorce, particularly cruelty and desertion. A judge could find "mental cruelty" in practically any antagonistic behavior he or she wanted, and "constructive desertion" even when a couple continued to live under the same roof. But in 1970 California passed the first comprehensive no-fault divorce law. Divorce became possible on the grounds of incurable insanity or "irreconcilable differences, which have caused the irremediable breakdown of the marriage."[29] Soon other states followed. New no-fault statutes permitted divorce where there were "irreconcilable differences" between the spouses or "irretrievable breakdown" of the marriage. Today, only South Dakota still requires that fault be shown before a divorce will be granted.[30]

Whether the movement to no-fault laws was a good idea or not is hotly debated. Since the law was changed, the divorce rate has climbed (although it has now leveled off and even begun to decline).[31] Undoubtedly, the new laws are partly to blame. By greatly reducing the formal barriers to divorce, no-fault statutes have allowed marriages to dissolve which would have stayed together under a fault-based law. At the same time, the new laws have reduced the strife and pain involved in many divorces that would have occurred under either system.[32] Moreover, much of the increased incidence of divorce is due to changes in moral values about marriage and divorce which predated the new laws and are not attributable to them. Our best hope for reducing the divorce rate lies in changing those values.

Some blame no-fault laws for diminishing the divorcing parties' sense of personal responsibility for their conduct, and thus for eroding public attitudes toward marriage as a lifelong covenant. If the divorce is granted without regard to fault, goes the argument, then no one feels responsible for having caused it. But the law is a very crude means for assigning responsibility. The causes of the breakup of a marriage are usually much more complicated than what the fault-based grounds for a divorce would imply. One instance of infidelity or cruelty may mask a long history of failures by both spouses. To the extent that a fault-based system makes it easy to blame one spouse entirely for the breakup because of some matrimonial offense, a fault-based system is misleading. Moreover, there is no necessary reason why responsibility for the breakup of a marriage still should not be felt under the newer laws.

Regardless of how one concludes this debate, no-fault divorce laws are here for the foreseeable future. It would be politically impossible today to revert to older laws.

Reducing Divorce's Devastation

Yet divorce can be permitted without being encouraged, endorsed or presented as being on a moral par with keeping the marital covenant. Just as the state licenses marriages, it also grants divorces. It can and should require something more than the simple immediate desire of the parties to be divorced. Laws that demand waiting periods, efforts at mediation and reconciliation, counseling and a court appearance, signal the state's disapproval of divorce and probably prevent some divorces. The importance of marriage as an institution in our society justifies these modest limits on the freedom to divorce.[33]

This justification especially applies when the couple seeking divorce has children who are minors. Divorce is devastating for children.

Substantial empirical evidence from the field of psychology now establishes that parental separation has substantial, long-term negative effects on children. These effects arise from the anxiety a child experiences when he or she is separated from a parent, from the conflict between parents that often occurs when they separate, and from the reduced influence of the noncustodial parent, generally the father, on the child.[34]

The negative effects of parental separation tend to produce children with lower self-esteem, decreased ability to defer gratification, and loss of ambition. These in turn lead to discipline problems and failure in school, use of drugs, and premarital sex. Not surprisingly, these problems have grown dramatically with higher divorce rates.[35]

The state can and should adopt laws which protect the interests of children in divorce, laws which are more stringent than those applicable to couples without children. Cochran and Vitz have proposed such child-protective divorce laws.[36] They make four recommendations to prevent, or minimize, the separation of children from their parents upon divorce.

First, where a husband and wife have living minor children, the law should require a one-year waiting period before granting a no-fault divorce.

Second, judges should be able to call on experts from fields other than law (such as psychology) to help ascertain what custodial arrangements would be in the best interests of the child.

Third, the law should protect the child's need for substantial contact with both parents by approving joint custody when the parents are able to agree to it. When they are not able to agree, the courts should award substantial visitation rights to the noncustodial spouse.[37] When the parents are separated but not divorced, the law should establish minimum standards of parental visitation and child support, both of which would help maintain contact with the noncustodial parent. Failure to allow the minimum amount of visitation or to provide the minimum amount of child support would be a violation of the law.

Fourth, the parents should be required to attempt to mediate child custody and visitation disputes prior to litigation. This reduces the amount of parental conflict to which the children are exposed. It encourages joint custody and more visitation, and it preserves parental autonomy and keeps decisions in the hands of those who presumably know the children's needs best—their parents.

Divorce laws should also seek to promote fair economic arrangements for all parties. Again, the needs of minor children should be paramount. Courts should attempt to divide the couple's property and assets and to require payments of alimony and child support in a way which allows everyone to maintain a standard of living as close as possible to what they enjoyed before the divorce. Unfortunately, it usually is impossible to keep everyone at that same level, since the divided family has greater total living expenses. But neither the husband nor wife nor children should bear a disproportionate share of any financial sacrifice.

Discriminating against Women and Children
Too often, however, divorce is a financial boon for men and a disaster for women and children. Incomes of women drop by an average of 73% after divorce, while those of men rise by an average of 42%.[38] In 1983, over one-third of single-parent families headed by women were poor, compared to less than one-seventh

of those headed by men.[39] This disparity is partly due to the lower incomes of working women in general, which is in turn attributable to employment discrimination, their relative lack of work experience, and their concentration in "pink ghetto" occupations. But part of the reason lies with divorce laws which systematically impoverish many women.

One aspect of this unjust system is the definition of a couple's *property*. The courts usually divide homes, furnishings, cars and bank accounts. But the court order frequently ignores other equally important assets, such as pensions or medical insurance, provided by a husband's career. By mutual consent, the wife has obviously contributed to these by working within their home and caring for their children. Reporting on a ten-year study of divorce in California after its no-fault law was passed in 1970, Stanford sociologist Lenore J. Weitzman concluded:

> If these assets are left out of the definition of property and the pool of property then the courts cannot simply be dividing property either equally or equitably. It's like saying we're going to divide the family jewels, but first we're going to give the husband all the diamonds. The diamonds are often his career assets, his pension, his license, his education, his earning capacity, his medical insurance and the other benefits of employment.[40]

The value of these contributions by the spouse (especially older women) must be considered when courts consider property division, alimony and child support.

A second reason for the poor position of women after divorce is that even when a court orders equitable child support and alimony payments, men frequently neglect these obligations. And courts often fail to enforce them. According to a survey by the Census Bureau, only 46% of the four million women with child support orders in 1983 received the full authorized amount. Another one-fourth received partial payments. One-fourth received nothing at all! Less educated and nonwhite women were less likely to have court orders and less likely to collect. In all, over three billion dollars went unpaid in 1983. This neglect of responsibility by fathers pushed 80,000 families below the official poverty line.[41]

Recent efforts have been made to find nonsupporting fathers and make them pay. Under a federal law that took effect on October 1, 1985, states will lose federal funds if they do not create mechanisms to withhold child support from paychecks after a parent falls one month behind in making payments. States must also attach state tax refunds and place liens on the property of delinquent spouses.[42] These actions should be continued. Fathers have a moral obligation to their children. Indeed tougher enforcement may even deter some divorces.

Parents, Children and the State

Few compelling state interests justify intervention into the privacy of the family. Aside from regulating marriage and divorce and stopping the physical abuse of a spouse, the state should not intervene in families without minor children.

When minor children are present, the state has a larger, but still limited role in family life. The authority of parents over their children comes from God, not the state. Parental authority is essential for their children's psychological well-being and for their growth into responsible adults. The state is unable to provide an adequate substitute for parental affection and authority. Even if it could, state child-rearing would be inconsistent with democratic government. Therefore, the presumption of public policy should always be that a child's best interests are served by preserving the relationships with his or her parents. In almost all situations, parents care for children better than the state.

Of course, parents can waive their parental rights and ask for state assistance. This may involve nothing more than state-supported counseling for parents or children. Or it may involve asking the state to make important decisions about the children's future (for example, when one or both parents request the state to determine their children's custody after a separation or divorce; when both parents, or the only custodial parent, request the state to terminate their custody rights over their children; or when the parents die or disappear without making any arrangements for their children's custody or care).

Where there is gross abuse or neglect, the state rightly intervenes against the parents' wishes. To protect the interests of children, the state may remove children from the parents' custody or order medical care which parents have refused. While parents should have the right to raise their children as they see fit, free from state intrusion, that right is not, nor should it be, absolute.[43] In order to assert its power to overrule parental authority, the state must show that the parents are unfit, unable or unwilling to care for their child adequately. This includes the infliction of, or repeated failure to prevent, serious bodily harm of one's child, including any form of sexual abuse. It would also include a refusal by the parents to authorize medical care necessary to preserve life.

Having a precise definition of the grounds for state intervention is essential. This gives fair warning to parents and prevents the state from overreaching its legitimate authority. One particular danger is that abuse and neglect statutes be written so broadly or enforced so loosely that the state can impose white, middle-class standards for child care and household management on parents who may have a different, but not necessarily inferior, set of values. Peter and Brigitte Berger write:

In the great majority of these cases children are taken away from their parents for alleged neglect or abuse of a nonphysical kind. This fact becomes especially grave when class, ethnic, and racial facts are taken into account. When the term "neglect" is applied to poor families, it commonly refers to quite elusive matters: Homes are deemed to be "dirty," nutrition to be "substandard" or "not wholesome" or (even more elusively) parents are found to be "non-caring" or "hostile." Sociologically, one must ask here to what extent such judgments involve application of upper-middle-class and white values to social strata with different values. Beyond this, one must ask whether the "standards" of the white upper-middle-class, and more specifically its professional component, are really so superior (not to mention "scientifically" supported) that the state should impose them coercively on the rest of the population. These questions have been asked with particular animus by blacks and Hispanics. Since the majority of children in foster care belong to these racial minorities, the issue has become embroiled in racial animosity and politics.[44]

Before the state intervenes in a family on behalf of the children, it should be required to provide a stringent proof that a case of abuse or neglect exists. The Supreme Court apparently has agreed, stating that "clear and convincing evidence" must be shown before the state can remove a child from his or her natural parents.[45]

Biblical teaching on the family, tradition and a belief in limited government all support this model of the relationships between parents, children and the state. The state should presume that full parental control over minor children is in the children's best interests.[46] Only compelling circumstances dare override that presumption.

Children's Rights

Today, however, advocates of children's rights denounce this traditional approach as outmoded and oppressive. In an appeal to individual rights and egalitarianism, they compare children to racial minorities and women, and argue for their liberation from their parents.

Certainly children have rights. The state should seek to protect the life, health and welfare of children (even unborn children) just as we do for adults.[47] For example, juvenile courts should accord minors the protections of due process of law like those accorded adult criminal defendants—the right to know the charges against them, to confront and cross-examine the witnesses against them, to be represented by counsel and to remain silent.[48] Indeed, the state should protect them in ways it cannot protect adults (for example, by adopting more stringent rules against selling pornography to minors).[49]

It also makes some sense to talk about the individual rights and the independent status of adolescent children. (Christians have used this argument in insisting that religious speech by students in public high schools should have "equal access" with other forms of speech.[50]) As children grow toward adulthood they ought to receive increasing responsibility and freedom.

But these rights—free speech, free exercise of religion and due process of law—are secured against infringement by the state. The situation is quite different when a minor child asserts rights against parental control—for example, freedom from their parents' rules of conduct, or freedom to procure abortions or contraceptives without parental consent or knowledge. Transferring the concepts of democratic rule, egalitarianism and individual rights to the context of families raises a host of problems and is not in the best interests of the children themselves or the vitality of the family.

Implementing this broad concept of children's rights will inevitably weaken parental authority and make the family less likely to serve the psychological needs of children. The assertion of children's rights also carries with it the further danger of state control of child-rearing. That is frequently the only alternative to parental care. As long as children lack the knowledge and capacity to care for themselves, they will be dependent on some adults. The only question is whether the adults to whom they submit will be their parents or professionals working at a state-run institution.[51] The presumption should favor the parents whenever possible. Only if there is gross abuse or neglect should the state intervene—through traditional legal means.

The state should not require that families resemble democracies. That presumes an equality among adults and children that does not exist. The law has long recognized that children are incapable of taking care of themselves. Indeed, that is the justification for state intervention on behalf of children. That reality undercuts the notion that children should be made autonomous and given freedom to make important decisions about their lives without parental advice, knowledge or control.[52]

Contraceptives and Abortions for Minors

The most controversial of these issues has been the access of abortion and state-funded contraceptives to minor children without their parents' consent or even knowledge. One can argue that sexually active adolescents have already rejected their parents' control. Therefore requiring parental involvement will only worsen the situation. Minors will be sexually active without contraceptives, thus increasing the number of unwanted pregnancies and abortion. On the other hand, it is precisely in such circumstances that minors most need their parents' support and counsel.

The Supreme Court has ruled that a state cannot give parents an "absolute, and possibly arbitrary" veto power over their minor child's decision to obtain an abortion. But the Court has approved a requirement that physicians "notify, if possible," the parents of a dependent minor.[53] The Court has yet to rule on the question of parental consent over the use of contraception by their children, but lower courts have struck down federal rules aimed at that.[54]

I believe parental consent should be required in both of these cases for all unmarried minor children who are dependent on their parents' support. The requirement of parental consent is a reasonable way for the state to strengthen the family and increase the likelihood that such crucial decisions will not be made hastily and immaturely. Certainly some parents will fail to act with love, compassion and wisdom. On balance, however, I believe they will be far more likely than state-funded professionals to act in the best interests of their children. To eliminate parental control of contraception and abortion decisions by their children sets a dangerous precedent for the further withdrawal of parent's rights over their children. It will also erode the sense of responsibility which parents have for their children.[55]

Publicly Funded Day Care

For similar reasons, I believe a vastly increased system of publicly funded day-care centers would be a mistake. Certainly some day-care is needed—for one-parent and low-income families who choose financial independence over welfare. Some families are simply unable to make it on one income. Unfortunately, employers and unions often increase the problem by limiting our choice to full-time employment or full-time parenting. Churches and synagogues are probably the best institutions to provide this care for those in their communities who truly need it. But even the best professional day-care center is a poor second best to care by most mothers and fathers at home. The inevitably high turnover rate of staff makes impossible the kind of emotional bonding with the caretakers comparable to that with parents whose constant presence provides security and trust.

Tragically, today's materialistic values often lead both parents of young children to choose to work full-time outside the home when they do not need to for financial reasons. At a minimum, government policy (via tax laws or public day-care programs) should not compound the problem and subsidize selfish choices. It is outrageous that current law discourages full-time parenting. A tax credit is available to offset child-care expenses if both parents work. But there is no tax credit if a couple decides that one of them should stay at home to promote the best possible nurture and care for the next generation. The biggest users of this credit are affluent families, not poor families with only one parent or those who truly need a second income. This provision should be rewritten at least to accord equal treatment to both options, or else should be eliminated except for poor families who truly need its benefit.[56]

Parents and the Public Schools

Christian parents often lament the problems of modern public schools. They complain that the schools teach their children values which conflict with their faith. With the development of the modern system of public education, parents surrendered to the schools a large amount of power over the socialization of their children. As long as the values taught in the schools (both by teachers and the youth culture) reflected those of the parents, the problem remained concealed. But in recent decades, the moral values of both the youth culture and professional educators increasingly have conflicted with those of parents.

For example, the supposedly neutral values of the moral education movement led by Lawrence Kohlberg involves the basic liberal assumption that tolerance toward everything is the only absolute norm.[57] One critic of modern public education argues that a "powerful axis of educators, policymakers, and pundits of the media" have sought to supplant the family in socializing children. This elite group has judged modern families—especially poor families—inadequate for this task.[58]

What can be done to reassert family control over education? At the very least, sex education and other values-clarification courses must clearly and sympathetically present biblical values as one option. Indeed, they should explain that historically this option has been the foundation of Western society. The omission of religion and religious values from the discussion communicates that they are unimportant matters in life and not worth serious consideration. That is anything but neutral! Christian parents should argue for review of their children's entire curriculum to insure fairness to Christian values. Do the textbooks mention the Christian faith which has motivated important historical figures?

Are believers pictured sympathetically or caricatured in the stories that children are reading? Just as women and minorities have pushed for curricular changes to erase stereotypes from textbooks, so should Christians. The goal is not to "Christianize" the curriculum. That would be unfair in schools serving all families. Rather the goal is truth and fairness.[59]

For parents who wish to include religion in their children's education, other possibilities are open within our present system of public schools. Christian parents often overlook "released time" religious instruction. Yet it is a perfectly constitutional way for Christians to provide religious instruction for their children while sending them to public schools. Under such a program, students who choose to participate are released from their regular school for a specified period each week to attend religious classes off school grounds.[60]

A second alternative is Christian instruction outside regular school hours to provide Bible study and a Christian perspective on the subjects studied in school. Churches or groups of parents can provide this education at the church or perhaps on rented school property.[61]

Third, the Supreme Court has specifically stated that objective teaching about religion is perfectly constitutional.[62] Obviously classes on the Bible as literature or comparative world religions will never replace Christian education, but they do affirm that religion is important and worth studying, and do present opportunities for children to gain some biblical knowledge in an age when ignorance of the Bible, even among churchgoers, is widespread.[63]

Another important way to help parents educate their children as they wish in public schools is to give them a choice of schools. A number of cities are using "magnet schools"—distinctive schools organized around a subject (for example, science or arts) or an approach to education (for example, innovative or traditional). Parents can voluntarily send their children to the school of their choice. The Constitution would not allow a Christian magnet school, of course. But one alternative school could adopt a curriculum that makes a particular effort to be fair to Christian values, presents objective study about religion, affirms the importance of religious values in life, and allows released-time education. More generally, by allowing individual schools to cater to a smaller spectrum of the community and by providing parents a choice, the creation of a diversity of public schools would enhance the parental role in education.[64]

The Voucher System

Vouchers would give parents even greater choice and control in their children's education.[65]

Public education today often resembles a vast monopolistic system controlled not by parents or even local school boards, but huge teachers' unions, state legislatures and bureaucrats. Uniformity across communities or even states is increasingly the rule. Financial uniformity is good, since it eliminates gross disparities in resources committed to public education in different parts of a state or metropolitan area. For too long children in poor neighborhoods have attended inferior schools. But uniformity in curriculum, textbooks and teaching methods makes public education a monopolistic system which gives parents little voice. Only wealthy families or those prepared to make enormous financial sacrifices can escape this system. A return to local control—and parental control—is essential.[66]

A voucher system would give public education dollars to parents instead of schools. Parents would receive a voucher for each school-age child. The voucher would pay for enrollment at any approved school the parents choose. In order to promote equality of opportunity in such a scheme, a sliding scale is essential so that poor families or those with handicapped children received more (at least $2,000 more) per child.

Certainly there would be enormous upheaval and some abuse.

But the state could set minimum standards for all participating schools and oversee advertising and consumer education. This would insure stable, quality schools and enable parents to make informed choices and protect them from unscrupulous entrepreneurs.

Perhaps the most serious problem would be the danger of social fragmentation. But it would be possible to establish a basic curriculum that would include things like American history and government. In any case, students in existing private schools have not seemed less American than their public-school counterparts. The experience of other nations confirms this. "Social and national unity does not rest, it appears, upon operating a single educational system."[67]

There would be a flood of new schools—by Christians, Jews, Muslims and, yes, even secular humanists. (In fact this would be an excellent way to show the secular intelligentsia, so dominant in professional educational circles, how few people really want secular humanist values taught to their children!) Present public schools could also continue for parents who wish to use them. In rural areas, they would probably continue much as they are today.

Education costs might decrease, and quality likely would increase, as schools competed for students. But far more important, power would be decentralized and the poorest would be empowered. The schools would again become responsible to parents. The increased power over their children's future would be enormous for all parents, perhaps especially for inner-city minorities who rightly feel powerless.[68] Most crucial of all would be the new social power and respect for the family.

Although most of our discussion has dealt with strengthening the family in the area of child-raising, the same principles apply to parallel areas. Under normal circumstances, the family (nuclear and extended) is also the best place to care for the sick, handicapped and elderly. Rather than turn more and more responsibilities over to professionals funded by government, we should give families the necessary financial help to handle these needs. Care in the family will usually be both more personal and less expensive. We could design a system of financial allowances plus professionals as a back-up rather than a substitute for the family.[69]

Economic Policy and the Family

Economic structures should support the family.[70] The U. S. Catholic bishops are right when they insist that high unemployment is destructive and immoral. It destroys families.[71]

A secure economic base is as essential for stable families today as it was in early Israel. To say that government policy should have this goal is not to promote state ownership or a perpetual system of welfare dependency. Wherever temporary public assistance is necessary, it must be designed to avoid dependency and strengthen both the nuclear and extended family. It certainly should not penalize the presence of fathers in the home!

Public policy designed to promote economically independent, self-sufficient families would mean strengthening the family farm, empowering each family to own their own house and drastically reducing unemployment.

A pro-family housing policy would use a more carefully targeted housing subsidy than the present tax deduction on interest and property taxes for homeowners. It might subsidize mortgages for poor families, and young families buying their first home. Or these families could be allowed to have tax-free savings accounts (like Individual Retirement Accounts), which could only be used toward a home purchase.[72]

Public policy can also assist families economically with child-raising, without giving the state control or creating incentives that harm children. As we saw earlier, the tax code should not subsidize day care more than care by a parent at home. The tax deduction could be converted to a tax credit to help families with children afford the costs of child-rearing, and to help more families keep one parent at home.[73] This would in effect constitute a government subsidy for each taxpaying family with children.

A comprehensive child subsidy program should also incorporate cash payments for poor families who would not receive the full tax credit because they pay little or no taxes. The United States is the only industrialized nation in the West which does not grant all families some sort of family allowance or child allowance—for instance, a periodic cash payment to families for each child. Both liberals and conservatives alike have supported such a mechanism of economic support for all families.[74] It would help poor families without encouraging the desertion of one parent or discouraging work.

State assistance with child-rearing might also include maternity and paternity leaves paid by the government. Many European countries provide such assistance. Just as society acknowledges its obligation to support the aged, the unemployed and dependents of deceased workers, it ought to acknowledge its responsibility for those who raise the next generation of citizens.[75] Loss of income from staying home to care for children is a serious burden for many families, but the benefits go to society as a whole. Public assumption of some of the burden seems justified.

Feminism and the Family
Many denounce feminism as anti-family. Certainly there are secular feminists who condemn heterosexual marriage as inherently oppressive. The push for the equality of women's rights, which emphasizes individual rights—and frequently individual economic advancement—can come at the expense of duties and obligations which individuals owe to one another, particularly in families. Sociologists Brigitte and Peter Berger write:

> Feminist causes come into conflict with the family as increasing numbers of women seek or are compelled to seek careers outside the home, and when in consequence family obligations come to be perceived as obstacles to self-realization in those careers. Individual women will have to decide on their own

priorities. Our own hope is that many will come to understand that life is more than a career and that this "more" is above all to be found in the family. But however individual women decide, they should not expect public policy to underwrite and subsidize their life plans.[76]

The same argument applies to men who seek fulfillment in their careers at the expense of their families. The problem is hyperindividualism, not equality of women's rights. Neither women nor men should expect subsidization of their selfishness. Too frequently, women alone are blamed for the push for abortion rights and state-supported child care, when in fact these are symptoms of a larger selfish individualism that knows no sexual boundary. The irony is that feminists often echo the values of the male-dominated culture which they have condemned, a culture which has de-emphasized family needs and responsibilities in favor of self-fulfillment largely through the consumption of material goods.

That said, public policy should not tolerate, and certainly not impose, unequal burdens on women. In fact, inequality, especially in the economic realm, is all around us. Earlier we noticed the economic problems that divorce creates for women. Despite federal statutes against sex discrimination in employment, grossly unequal pay for women persists.[77] They earn about sixty per cent of what men do, even in comparable jobs. As women gain more experience and education, their relative position should rise, but it will not disappear without some legal reform.[78]

Would the proposed Equal Rights Amendment (ERA) help or hinder a pro-family agenda? I think it would help. There is no contradiction between strong families and respect for the equality of women. Biblical faith demands both. The ERA says:

Section 1. Equality of rights under the law shall not be denied or abridged by the United States or by any State on account of sex.

Section 2. The Congress shall have the power to enforce, by

appropriate legislation, the provisions of this article.

Since a similar Pennsylvania law has been used to defend the right to public funding of abortion, it would be very important to include a rider to the amendment that clearly prevents this.[79] Similarly, an acceptable rider would also need to be added to exclude the possibility that the amendment could be used to demand that government grant gay marriages legal status.[80]

Public policy cannot save the family. But it could and should strengthen marriages and parents rather than undermine them. Demanding the necessary changes to guarantee that government actions promote the wholeness and shalom of the family is one essential element of a consistent pro-life agenda for today.

Part 4

NUCLEAR WEAPONS

Chapter 8

Christian Faith and the Nuclear Arms Race

Christians approach the problems of war and peace with fear and reverence. God is the Lord of life, and so each human life is sacred; modern warfare threatens the obliteration of human life on a previously unimaginable scale.[1]
U.S. Conference of Catholic Bishops

The next two decades are the most dangerous in human history. Admiral Hyman G. Rickover is the father of the U.S. nuclear navy. When he retired in 1982, he warned that unless we abandon nuclear weapons, we will destroy ourselves. In January 1983, I did a two-day seminar at a Christian College with Dr. Delmar Bergen, the head of nuclear-weapons testing at Los Alamos National Laboratory. Dr. Bergen said that the probability of nuclear war in the next ten to twenty-five years was almost 100%.

At any moment they choose, the leaders of the United States and the USSR could order the ultimate abortion. A major nuclear war would murder hundreds of millions of people, destroy civilization as we know it, and make vast sections of the planet uninhabitable.

Year by year as we stockpile more and more conventional and nuclear weapons, one billion people live in agonizing poverty. Thirty-five thousand die every day of starvation. The nations of the world devote as much money each year (about $600 billion in 1982) to military expenditures as the poorest one-half of the world's people have as total income. The arms race is truly, as Pope Paul VI said, an act of aggression against the poor.[2] If all human life is inestimably precious, then pro-life Christians dare not ignore a runaway arms race which robs the poor of life.

A Biblical Call to Peace

War kills persons created in the image of God (Gen 1:27). War kills persons so precious to God that his only Son died for them on a Roman cross (Jn 3:16). God's special love for persons, revealed in creation and redemption, is the first reason Christians are peacemakers.

To say that war is evil because human life is inestimably precious, however, is not to say that life itself is the highest good. Obedience to God is more important than life. It is right to risk death to share the gospel. It is right to risk death to protect the innocent, preserve freedom and seek justice for the poor. Kenneth Kantzer is surely correct in an editorial in *Christianity Today:*

> I value my freedoms of speech and press and religion more than life. To teach my children about God is more important to me than life itself. I would rather not bring children into the world than to give them birth only to have them reared as Marxist atheists.[3]

Biblical Christians disagree over whether it is right to kill for the sake of justice and freedom.[4] But all Christians committed to the sacredness of human life agree that it is right to risk death to protect and share life.

Those who know the Author of life and believe his claim to be the resurrection and the life have no fear of embracing this paradox. They willingly risk their own lives in order to share life more abundantly with their neighbors. And abundant life is first of all a living relationship with God in Christ which leads to eternal life, and then that fullness of shalom promised in the Scriptures.

Nowhere is the biblical call to peacemaking clearer than in the messianic prophecies of shalom and their fulfillment in Jesus the Messiah. The prophets looked ahead to the "latter time" (the messianic age) when the boot of the trampling warrior and the battle garments rolled in blood would disappear (Is 9:5). When the child who is the Prince of Peace comes, it can be said: "Of the increase of his government and of peace there will be no end" (Is 9:6-7; compare also Is 11:6, 9). The messianic hope anticipates the time when "they shall beat their swords into plowshares, and their spears into pruning hooks; nation shall not lift up sword against nation, neither shall they learn war any more" (Is 2:4; Mic 4:3).

The early church declared Jesus to be the fulfillment of these messianic prophecies. Matthew 4:15-16 quotes Isaiah 9:1-2 in connection with the beginning of Jesus' proclamation of the coming of the messianic kingdom. Paul refers to Isaiah 11:1 and 10 in Romans 15:12. In Luke 1:68-79, Zechariah announces that John the Baptist will prepare the way for Jesus, the Messiah. Quoting Isaiah 9:2, Zechariah points with eager anticipation to the Messiah who will "guide our feet into the way of peace" (Lk 1:79). When the angels announce Jesus' birth with the choral shout "peace among men" (Lk 2:14), they simply confirm the fulfillment of the prophetic vision of messianic peace.

In his life and teaching, Jesus did bring shalom in all its fullness. He claimed authority to forgive sins and then died as the atonement for sin in order to bring sinners into right relationship with a holy God. By caring for the poor and needy, he brought shalom into economic life. By transcending sexual prejudice and treating women as persons, he brought shalom to social life. By healing the sick and cleansing the lepers, he brought wholeness to the least of human society.

Nowhere is Jesus' call to be peacemakers clearer than in his radical extension of neighbor love to include even enemies.

You have heard that it was said, "You shall love your neighbor and hate your enemy." But I say to you, Love your enemies and pray for those who persecute you, so that you may be sons of your Father who is in heaven; for he makes his sun rise on the evil and on the good, and sends rain on the just and on the unjust. For if you love those who love you, what reward have you? Do not even the tax collectors do the same? And if you salute only your brethren, what more are you doing than others? Do not even the Gentiles do the same? You, therefore, must be perfect, as your heavenly Father is perfect. (Mt 5:43-47)

Traditional Jewish thought had largely limited the obligation of neighbor love to fellow Israelites.[5] Jesus extends it to everyone in need, even our enemies. And he grounds this astonishing demand in the very character of the Father who showers the goods of creation on both the just and the unjust. Since that is the way of the Father, peacemakers are blest children of God (Mt 5:9).

Whether Jesus' call to his disciples to love their enemies excludes participation in war has long been debated. Most Christians for three hundred years thought so.[6] Since the time of St. Augustine, however, a majority of Christians have believed that reluctantly, in carefully limited circumstances, love for neighbor demands taking up arms to protect the innocent. The messianic kingdom of peace has truly begun with the life, death and resurrection of Jesus. But it is not yet here in its fullness. Only at Christ's return will the prophecies of messianic peace be perfectly fulfilled. Until then, it is argued, war may sometimes be justified, although it is always horribly evil.

That is not to say that Christians dare ever set aside Jesus' call to love enemies. Only if the cause is just and the war is fought with love for enemies dare Christians kill. Over the centuries, as Christians have struggled to develop this attitude toward war, the just war tradition has slowly taken shape.

Most Christians today stand in that tradition. Therefore, it is imperative to apply the criteria of the just war tradition to the arms race, especially the nuclear arms race.

The Just War Tradition and Nuclear Weapons

To be justified, according to the just war tradition, a war must (1) be a last resort; (2) have a just cause; (3) have right intentions (restoration of a just peace); (4) begin after a prior declaration of war; (5) have a reasonable chance of success. Furthermore, the war itself must be fought in a way that respects (1) noncombatant immunity from direct and intentional attack (it is murder to aim at civilians); and (2) proportionality (the good results of the war or any specific engagement must outweigh the evils involved).

Would it ever be justified, according to these criteria, to use nuclear weapons whether in a massive retaliatory strike against population centers or a more limited attack on military and industrial targets? (Later, I will examine the interesting suggestion that we dare never use nuclear weapons but should continue to possess them.)

Is there a reasonable chance of winning a nuclear war? Could we preserve through nuclear war the peaceful, productive societies, democratic processes and freedom and liberty that we rightly treasure? According to the just war tradition it is wrong to fight even if one's cause is just if there is no reasonable chance of success.

Almost everything we seek to defend would be destroyed in a major nuclear war. The U.S. Office of Technology Assessment indicates that a large attack against military and industrial targets would kill 70-160 million Americans and 100 million folk in the Soviet Union.[7] If population centers were targeted, the death toll would reach as high as 190 million Americans and 130 million Soviets. Most hospitals would be destroyed. Severe burn cases would be in the tens of millions as would excruciatingly painful deaths from radiation. Food would become scarce or unavailable. Starvation would become epidemic worldwide. According to a U.S. government study, 65%-90% of the industrial capacity of both nations would be destroyed. In response to the anarchy and desperation, any remaining governmental structures would quickly feel compelled to adopt totalitarian measures to preserve a modicum of order. Cherished freedoms and democratic institutions would disappear in the aftermath of a major nuclear war. There is no reasonable chance of winning a massive nuclear exchange.

But what about the increasingly accepted notion of fighting a limited nuclear war with only specific military installations targeted? If it stayed very limited, there might be a reasonable chance of success. But that is a huge if. Former U.S. Secretary of Defense Harold Brown rejects the notion that any nuclear exchange would remain limited.

> To me it seems very unlikely, almost to the point of impossibility. . . . It is much more likely . . . that it would escalate to larger and larger exchanges that would end up in an all-out thermonuclear war that would destroy both countries.[8]

Escalation could occur in a vast number of ways: computer failure, unforeseen effects of nuclear blasts, a desperate attempt to avoid defeat, or human irrationality in a situation of nearly total panic and chaos. In 1975 the United States Arms Control and Disarmament Agency (ACDA) pointed to possible unforeseen developments in the course of an actual nuclear exchange. In earlier nuclear tests, it was discovered that high-altitude bursts "wiped out long-distance radio communications for hours at distances up to 600 miles from the burst point."[9] What would happen if the soldiers in nuclear submarines and ICBM silos could not communicate with headquarters for hours at the height of a nuclear crisis? The ACDA also noted that earlier tests showed that electromagnetic pulses from a blast can play havoc with the electrical equipment (such as computers) that controls the nuclear arms.[10] Only at our peril dare we ignore the ACDA's warning that many unforeseen dangers could arise during the course of limited nuclear war.

Escalation could occur in other ways. Whoever appeared to be losing a limited nuclear war might become desperate.

> Once the threshold of atomic weaponry is crossed in battle, the pressure for use of "just one higher level" of atomic force will

be practically irresistible. The side badly hurt by atomic artillery shells will respond by dropping medium sized atomic bombs on the offending artillery enplacements. The answer to that will be larger bombs or medium range missiles against the airfields from which the tactical atomic strikes come. Quickly the side less equipped with tactical nuclear weapons . . . will feel pressed to resort to thermonuclear attack.[11]

Bryan Hehir, a leading Catholic ethicist, concludes that we must understand the psychological dynamic of our situation. Any use of nuclear weapons makes it psychologically easier to move to a higher level of nuclear exchange. Therefore, we must have an ethical "firebreak" between the use of conventional and nuclear weapons. Even if tactical nuclear weapons could be justified in terms of the criteria of discrimination and proportionality, they dare not be used because of the psychological danger of escalation.[12]

Furthermore, strategic planners who foresee a rationally controlled, calculated nuclear exchange that comes to a reasonable halt after ten or twenty million casualties must have a naive view of human nature. According to the Christian view of persons, sinful people often choose evil things even under the best of circumstances. Is it probable that human rationality would remain in control during intense confusion, panic, misinformation and anger?

The criterion of a reasonable chance of success raises severe doubts about the moral justification of any use of nuclear weapons.

What about the principle of noncombatant immunity? According to the just war tradition, it is murder to intentionally target civilians. The long-standing Western policy of a massive retaliatory strike against the Soviet Union would do precisely that. Most Christian ethicists, however, would agree with Ken Kantzer and John Stott that it is immoral to aim nuclear weapons at civilians. Therefore we must reject the policy of massive retaliation.

We should pledge that we will not aim our nuclear warheads

at civilian populations—no matter what the provocation. . . .
We should renounce any retaliations in kind, even for an opponent's bombing of our civilian population. It is always wrong
to intend to kill the innocent.[13]

United States government officials, however, told the U.S. Catholic
bishops working on their major study of the nuclear question that
the United States does not specifically target Soviet cities or civilians.[14] But we do target thousands of military targets in major
population centers. The U.S. strategic nuclear targeting plan has
sixty military targets in Moscow alone.[15] (Soviet strategy undoubtedly also has similar targets and is subject to the same moral
challenge.) United States government officials told the Catholic
bishops that "once any substantial number of weapons were used,
the civilian casualty levels would quickly become truly catastrophic, and that even with attacks limited to military targets, the
number of deaths in a substantial exchange would be almost in-
distinguishable from what might occur if civilian centers had been
deliberately and directly struck."[16]

Only in some very limited technical sense does attacking military targets meet the just war criterion of noncombatant immunity. To adopt a policy of aiming at thousands of military targets
in population centers with tens of millions of people violates the
spirit of noncombatant immunity.

Furthermore, it clearly runs contrary to a third major criterion:
proportionality. Do the good results (defending freedom) justify
the number of deaths estimated by the U.S. Office of Technology
Assessment? Would it be legitimate to kill up to 190 million Americans and 130 million Soviets in a nuclear exchange? Are those
means proportionate to the ends? Some Christians honestly think
so.[17] I disagree. In addition to hundreds of millions of Soviet and
American dead, there would be millions of deaths in Western and
Eastern Europe, China and elsewhere; long-term ecological dam-
age; even the danger of a nuclear winter. The principle of proportionality prohibits the use of nuclear weapons.

The other two criteria also point to the same conclusion. On the basis of the just war tradition, Christians must say no to the use of nuclear weapons.

Nuclear Weapons as a Deterrent

But rejecting the use of nuclear weapons need not demand rejecting their possession. No one in fact wants to *use* nuclear weapons. We possess them for the sake of deterrence so that they will never be used. The U.S. Catholic bishops, the pope and many Protestants conclude that it is justified, at least in the short run, to possess nuclear weapons if we make it clear that it would be immoral to use them.

How should we evaluate this position?

If one could be very certain that deterrence would continue to prevent nuclear war indefinitely, this position would be attractive. The prospect of Soviet totalitarianism encompassing the globe is truly terrifying. If we could be very certain nuclear deterrence would prevent this tragedy *without* leading to nuclear war, then living with deterrence might seem ethically defensible. In fact, it may be that we have come to live comfortably with the awful reality of nuclear weapons precisely because we believe we will never use them.

But this position seems profoundly problematic at three points. First, it tends to legitimize the arms race without checking it. Second, it destroys the credibility of deterrence by announcing that we will not really use nuclear weapons. And finally, it increases the risk of accidental nuclear war because of continued development and installation of nuclear weapons.

First, then, we must deal with the fact that no present government has indicated the slightest openness to accept the approach of "possession without use." Thus theologians who take this position end up offering a rationale for continuing possession of nuclear weapons (and the arms race) without changing the government's intent to *use* nuclear weapons. The practical effect, therefore, is to offer justification for the ongoing arms race.

Second, every public figure who comments on deterrence makes it clear that deterrence works only if the Soviets believe we will use nuclear weapons. Former U.S. Secretary of Defense Robert McNamara reflected that general view when he said: "It is the clear and present ability to destroy the attacker as a twentieth-century nation and an *unwavering* will to *use those forces in retaliation* for a nuclear attack that provides the deterrent."[18] Thus possession without use destroys the very deterrence one hopes to preserve.

The only way out would be to keep our intention not to use them a presidential secret. But that entangles everyone (except a handful of persons around the president) in the immoral position of preparing for what the just war tradition calls mass murder.

There is a third serious objection to this position. The validity of the stance rests on the assumption that continuing to possess nuclear weapons does not involve us in immoral risks. Unfortunately, the evidence would suggest otherwise. The risks of nuclear war increase year by year. We came to the very brink of nuclear holocaust during the Cuban missile crisis. In 1979 and 1980, computer failures resulted in three instances where the central U.S. command believed for three to six minutes that the Soviet Union had launched a nuclear attack. Republican Senator Barry Goldwater reported that the U.S. air defense system received 147 false alarms during a typical eighteen-month period.[19]

A chilling article in the *Bulletin of the Atomic Scientists* of November 1980 shows how human error could lead to a nuclear catastrophe. Because of emotional problems, drug use and so on, about five thousand military personnel already working with the U.S. nuclear-weapons program are removed every year. One army code specialist reported: "Missile soldiers sometimes were high when they attached nuclear warheads to the missiles. So were soldiers who connected the two pieces up to make the missile operational."[20] No one reading this carefully documented article can feel any optimism about indefinitely avoiding nuclear war.

The pace of technological change also tends to destabilize the situation and undermine deterrence. Both sides mistrust each other. Both fear the other may make a technological breakthrough that would give "the enemy" a significant advantage. Therefore, both continue feverishly to develop ever more sophisticated, ever more deadly nuclear weapons. And a major technological breakthrough could make things even more dangerous. One country might be tempted to strike first while it possessed technological superiority. On the other hand, the elaborate spying networks of both sides almost guarantee that the other side would pick up enough information about the breakthrough to be exceedingly frightened—perhaps so frightened that it would strike before the other side made use of its advantage.

Robert McNamara was surely correct when he spoke of the "mad momentum intrinsic to the development of all new nuclear weaponry."[21] Every year that we continue the present policy of adopting new nuclear weapons as soon as technology makes them possible, we edge closer to the day when deterrence will fail. James Schlesinger, President Nixon's defense secretary, called for a limited war strategy precisely because he feared that deterrence *would* fail. To gamble on deterrence working indefinitely is to cling to an increasingly shaky reed.

With reluctance some concur with the U.S. Catholic bishops that deterrence may be accepted temporarily if we work hard at disarmament. Others doubt that the just war tradition permits any acceptance of nuclear deterrence. Both groups, however, agree that the just war tradition compels Christians to throw themselves vigorously into reversing the nuclear arms race.

Reversing the Nuclear Arms Race
Christians need to change public policy. To do that, however, they need to change public opinion. And a good place for Christians to start is with themselves—namely, the church. In evangelical

Protestant circles, two things are especially crucial.

First, we must reject and correct the kind of doctrinaire anticommunism which sees the Soviet people as atheistic enemies to be hated or even destroyed rather than as persons to be loved and understood. That does not mean that we ignore the terrible evils of Marxist totalitarianism, but we need to say no to that hostile mindset that sees Marxists almost as demons to be eliminated rather than as neighbors to be cared for. Of course, no responsible Christian leaders say that. But this sort of attitude is widespread at the popular level. And it is precisely this kind of attitude that hinders bilateral and multilateral disarmament.

Jesus taught us to love our enemies. The just war tradition has always insisted that even when we reluctantly decide we must use force to resist persons who do evil things, Jesus' command to love our enemies still applies. Loving our enemies at least means refusing to put them in the category of enemies to be hated or eliminated. It at least means refusing to put them in the category of subhuman beings whose lives are less important than ours. Loving our enemies means insisting that even the wicked are still persons for whom Christ died, neighbors to be loved and understood.

I am not denying that Soviet leaders have been and are totalitarian atheists (although we should be careful to distinguish the Marxist leaders from the Soviet people). But Jesus' command to love even our enemies means that even totalitarian Marxist leaders are neighbors whom Jesus Christ commands us to understand and love.

American evangelicals could make a significant contribution to American-Soviet understanding if we would cleanse our own community of this kind of unchristian anticommunism. We could promote a massive program of interaction and communication between the people of the United States and the Soviet Union. We could develop programs that would enable thousands of church leaders from both countries to visit sister churches in the other country. We could have a few thousand of our most gifted students from Christian colleges study in exchange programs in the USSR each year. Of course the Soviet government would try to manipulate such programs. But surely our free democratic society can handle these problems much better than their closed system.

Second, we need to take a clear stand against a certain kind of unbiblical eschatological speculation that destroys a concern for peacemaking. In popular evangelical circles there is a widespread view that Jesus Christ will certainly return in the next decade or two. Since he is returning so soon and since things will get worse and worse before he does, there is no obligation to work hard for nuclear disarmament.

Now I believe with all my heart that at some specific point in time, the Risen Lord Jesus will return and history as we know it will end. I believe in his bodily Second Coming. It may be today or tomorrow. It may be in five or five hundred years. The one thing that Jesus himself said he did not know was the day of his return (Mt 24:36). Beware of unbiblical Christians today who claim to know more than Jesus did.

In the New Testament, the blessed hope of Jesus' Second Coming always functioned as the ground for an ethical imperative to press on to do all that he had taught. It never functioned—or at least when it did the leaders of the church condemned it—as a cop-out to avoid Jesus' clear commands. First Corinthians 15:58 is typical. After a glorious chapter on Jesus' resurrection and our future resurrection at his return, Paul concludes: "Therefore . . . be steadfast, immovable, always abounding in the work of the Lord, knowing that in the Lord your labor is not in vain."

Almost all the other New Testament texts about the Second Coming end the same way. Because he is surely coming back, we must work even harder at all the things he commanded. He commanded us to care for the poor. He commanded us to spread the gospel throughout the whole world. He commanded us to be peacemakers. Of course there will be adultery and broken families, perhaps in increasing numbers, until Christ returns. But no-body concludes that that biblical warning means that we should stop trying to prevent adultery and divorce. Nor does the prediction of wars and rumors of wars mean that Christians should not ardently oppose the most terrible assault on God's good creation ever contemplated by humanity. Precisely because we know that the Master is coming back we should be busy doing all that he commanded until he returns.

It will not be church officials, however, but government leaders who will make the momentous decisions to use or abolish nuclear weapons. Shaping public policy on the nuclear arms race is therefore a moral necessity for all pro-life Christians.

What changes in public policy should Christians promote? The next chapter deals with that important question.

Chapter 9

Building Peace in the Nuclear Age

Peace is not just the absence of war. . . . Like a cathedral, peace must be constructed patiently and with unshakable faith.[1]
John Paul II

Peace is the fruit of order. Order in human society must be shaped on the basis of respect for the transcendence of God and the unique dignity of each person, understood in terms of freedom, justice, truth and love. To avoid war in our day we must be intent on building peace in an increasingly interdependent world.[2]
U.S. Catholic Bishops

B uilding peace in the nuclear age seems like an overwhelming task. But God has called us to be peacemakers and so we can expect the necessary grace and wisdom from God.

The challenge before Christians is to understand and evaluate the wide range of defense issues from a Christian perspective. In the last chapter, we examined the biblical call to peace. I argued, on the basis of the just war tradition, that we must say no to nuclear weapons. Nuclear weapons are *fundamentally* different from conventional weapons. As Bernard Brodie, one of the original nuclear strategists, has said, "We should understand the genuinely new nature of something not only instantaneously calamitous but wildly unpredictable, and very hard indeed to stop at any point short of grandiose, wanton destruction."[3] I also argued that not only the use but also the possession of nuclear weapons cannot be justified according to the just war criteria.

Not all Christians, of course, stand within the just war tradition. But the majority do. Consequently, this chapter is written from that perspective.[4] From a just war orientation, a nation has a right to national self-defense. Therefore, a number of just war Christian theorists believe the United States may need to strengthen conventional defenses if reliance on nuclear defense is immoral. If that route is taken, however, it is essential to heed the Catholic bishops' warning against "making the world safe for conventional war."[5] According to the just war tradition, conventional war can also be indiscriminate in conduct and disproportionate to any moral purpose. To develop that issue, however, would require another chapter (or book). Here the focus is on nuclear policy.

What practical proposals will foster nuclear disarmament? In the following pages I call for an improvement in U.S.-Soviet relations, a reassessment of military doctrine and strategy, and effective arms control leading to bilateral phased reductions. This approach has virtue because it recognizes that the problem is not merely one of technology and that the solution must go beyond changes in weaponry. Working our way out of the "nuclear box" requires changing our way of thinking about the role of military power and building international trust as we engage in bilateral and multilateral talks. I begin, therefore, with a look at the relationship between the United States and the Soviet Union.

The U.S.-Soviet Relationship

We are all very aware that the relationship between the United States and the Soviet Union is one of distrust and vast ideological difference. Central to the antagonism is the fact that the 1917 Russian Revolution installed a totalitarian, expansionist Marxist dictatorship. Its present shape, however, developed after World War 2. By late 1945 it was evident that the wartime alliance of the two nations had crumbled. American and Soviet interests collided as both powers sought to fill the vacuum left in post-war Europe. The United States and USSR each believed that they alone held the key to world peace and justice while the other embodied all things evil. Seweryn Bialer, an expert on Soviet affairs, describes the conflict this way:

> We are divided not only by our different interests as great powers but also and more importantly, by diverse values and beliefs to which we subscribe, by different historical experience, and by devotion to different systems and rules of behavior which are based on different principles and priorities of human existence, human values and political beliefs.[6]

Building peace must begin with an effort to neutralize and moderate superpower antagonisms. For Americans, this involves several steps. First, we need to look at ourselves. We must assess our own behavior and national attitudes and, as mentioned in the last chapter, correct the kind of rigid, doctrinaire anticommunism that produces ideological blindness. Second, we need to achieve a balanced understanding of Soviet purposes and policies. It is silly to be either overly euphoric or overly pessimistic about the relationship. Third, we must engage in a program of cooperation which will stimulate and sustain efforts on both sides to work for improved relations.[7] The words spoken by President Kennedy at American University in 1963 still ring true today: "Americans are neither omnipotent nor omniscient. . . . We must not see a distorted and desperate view of the other side; we must not see conflict as inevitable, accommodation as impossible, and communication as nothing more than an exchange of threats."[8]

Military Doctrine

Building peace in the nuclear age also entails a rethinking of military doctrine and strategy. If the analysis in the last chapter is correct, then we should move away from our dependence on nuclear weapons. A quick review of the evolution of U.S. nuclear doctrine shows that U.S. policy has moved in the opposite direction and shifted to war-fighting strategies that emphasize nuclear weapons. Such strategies are repugnant in and of themselves. They make a shambles of strategic deterrence since they make possible the use of nuclear weapons in other than defensive situations. And they increase our dependence on nuclear weapons, since the weapons become an integral part of these strategies. How did this change occur?

Deterrence was formally declared to be the first principle of American nuclear strategy in 1953. In varying forms, it has remained so ever since. The concept of deterrence is simply: prevention by threat.[9]

"Massive retaliation," adopted by President Eisenhower, was the original theory of deterrence which intended to "couple strategic nuclear forces to the deterrence of lesser as well as mortal [that is, nuclear] threats."[10] Eisenhower's secretary of state, John Foster Dulles, indicated in a 1954 speech that the United States would use nuclear weapons not only in response to a nuclear attack, but also in response to a wide range of Soviet actions.

President Kennedy moved away from exclusive reliance on massive retaliation in the 1960s. Instead, his policy of "flexible response" was designed to enable the United States to respond appropriately to any type and level of Soviet attack. This form of deterrence carried U.S. policy through the 1970s, although President Carter's Presidential Decision 59 (1979), permitting limited nuclear response, began to move U.S. policy beyond mere deterrence. This was denied, however, in the words of the then Secretary of Defense Harold Brown, "PD-59 does not assume that we can 'win' a limited nuclear war, nor does it intend or pretend to enable us to do so. It does seek both to prevent the Soviets from being able to win such a war and to convince them that they could not."[11]

Shortly thereafter, the move toward nuclear war-fighting strategies began in earnest. Admiral Eugene Carroll of the Center for Defense Information notes that the process began under President Carter, who saw the need to bolster his image on defense as the presidential election drew near.[12] The changes continued under President Reagan, and today implemented plans to build nuclear war-fighting capabilities have been matched by declared policy. In the Reagan Administration's first budget request to Congress, the new goal was stated as follows: "U.S. defense policies ensure our preparedness to respond to and, if necessary, successfully fight either conventional or nuclear war."[13] What a "successful" nuclear war means is hard to fathom. The clearest articulation of the new war-fighting strategy was contained in Secretary of Defense Weinberger's *Fiscal 1984-1988 Defense Guidance:*

> United States nuclear capabilities must prevail even under the condition of prolonged war. . . . Should deterrence fail and strategic nuclear war with the USSR occur, the United States must prevail and be able to force the Soviet Union to seek earliest termination of hostilities on terms favorable to the United States. . . . US strategic nuclear forces and their command and communications links should be capable of supporting controlled nuclear counterattacks over a protracted period while maintaining a reserve of nuclear forces sufficient for trans- and post-attack protection and coercion.[14]

The Reagan Administration maintains that this war-fighting strategy enhances deterrence because our growing arsenal presents any adversary with a greater threat of annihilation. However, many analysts believe that war-fighting doctrines erode deterrence.[15] Weinberger's own words quoted above indicate that war-fighting strategies are necessary "should deterrence fail." The increased production and deployment of new weapons and delivery systems (justified by war-fighting scenarios), which is occurring on both sides, makes the strategic balance more threatening and less stable. It is by no means certain that nuclear war-fighting scenarios and weapons have increased deterrence. More likely, they tempt leaders to lean toward a first-strike strategy.

Clearly, a re-evaluation is in order. In the previous chapter I argued that nuclear deterrence is immoral. Here we see how it has been undermined by the recent shift in military doctrine toward strategies of fighting and winning nuclear wars. We have increased rather than decreased our immoral dependence on nuclear weapons.

One important first step toward peace would be to withdraw all support from war-fighting and counterforce (or first-strike) strategies. A significant step in this direction would be for the United States to declare that it will not be the first to use nuclear weapons. (The policy of no first use is described in detail further on.) Such a step would promote further steps in arms control.

Nuclear Arms Control

Tragically, much of what is called "arms control" has actually served to legitimize the arms race. Further, many scholars such as Thomas Schelling believe that even the modestly successful arms-control efforts of earlier administrations have been derailed in recent years: "For several years what are called arms negotiations have been mostly a public exchange of accusations; and it often looks as if it is the arms negotiations that are driving the arms race."[16]

Nuclear arms control should be judged by whether or not it helps to achieve the following goals: reducing the number of nuclear weapons; helping to prevent the further spread of nuclear weapons; slowing or stopping the development and deployment of new nuclear weapons; enhancing stability and reducing uncertainty; reducing the cost of the military; and imposing qualitative limits on the development of destabilizing systems. In addition to these central criteria, we must also evaluate arms-control proposals in terms of negotiability and possible verification.

Specific concrete measures of nuclear arms control, of course, can succeed only if we also improve U.S.-Soviet relationships and rethink military strategy. But arms control can play a vital role in helping the world move away from the nuclear abyss. Part of its value is in the dialog itself; negotiations have served to reduce mistrust between the United States and USSR by increasing understanding of policies and perceived threats. It also provides the forum within which necessary changes in weaponry and deployment can take place. Thus it is to a discussion of concrete proposals for nuclear arms control that I now turn.

U.S. citizens should demand of our leaders steady progress in all forms of arms control: confidence-building measures, force restructuring, freezes, reductions and independent initiatives. Specifically, I advocate:

1. A declaration of a no first-use policy by the United States and NATO;

2. A restructuring of forces away from counterforce weapons;

3. A rejection of weapons in space;

4. A mutual, verifiable nuclear freeze (perhaps beginning with a partial freeze leading to reductions);

5. A resumption in negotiations for a comprehensive test ban;

6. A willingness to utilize independent, national initiatives.

Confidence-Building Measures

Confidence-building measures (CBMs) aim primarily to bolster stability by reducing the chance of accidents that might lead to war and by building confidence in the East-West strategic relationship. These measures should supplement other ongoing arms-control negotiations and efforts to improve U.S.-Soviet relations.

The precedent for CBMs was set in 1963 with the establishment of the Hot Line for high-level East-West communication in times of crisis. Other channels for increased dialog should also be explored. We should establish a joint crisis-management center and set up teleconferencing centers in both capitals for use by government officials whenever needed.[17] Such communication enhances stability by reducing uncertainty and clarifying superpower perceptions. Other forms of CBMs which should be explored include the following: exchanging inventory of strategic forces; safeguarding national monitoring capabilities; prohibiting interference with satellites and other means of verification; and discussing naval incidents and military exercises.

No First Use

One major initiative which would do much to bolster stability is the declaration of a no-first-use policy. Christians should call on the United States, along with NATO, to declare that it will not be the first to use nuclear weapons. Such a declaration would enhance stability. It is also consistent with the rejection of war-fighting strategies, of which first-use policy is one.

The policy of no first-use is not a new idea. It was first suggested at the 1955 Geneva summit meeting that France, the USSR, Great Britain and the United States refrain from a first-use of nuclear weapons against any country. Then, in 1964, China became the first nation to declare that it would not be the first to use nuclear weapons under any circumstances. The USSR made its formal pledge in 1982, but added that it would take into account whether other nations followed suit. The Soviets also hinted that changes in weapons deployment consistent with the pledge would be forthcoming. Doubts about the Soviet pledge abound because those changes have not occurred.

The United States has refrained from making a pledge of no first-use because of its promise to protect Western Europe. Since the early fifties, the United States has said it would be willing to use nuclear weapons first to counter a conventional Soviet attack against Western Europe. The United States claims that its willingness to use nuclear weapons in Europe demonstrates NATO's seriousness of purpose. Many Europeans view this policy as an effective deterrent because it raises the possibility of escalation to general nuclear war. The main argument against a pledge of no first-use, then, is that it would make war in Europe more likely because of the conventional superiority of the Warsaw Treaty Organization (WTO).

There is, however, a fundamental flaw in this logic. If NATO were to make a nuclear response to a conventional attack, it would be suicidal since the USSR would most likely retaliate with nuclear weapons. The danger of escalation, therefore, which some see as a strong deterrent, actually poses the greatest problem for Europe. This flaw is realized and exposed by European uneasiness whenever East-West tensions mount. In essence, Europe is in a no-win situation which could only be improved by a no first-use policy.

A basic question then is, What changes in weaponry and doctrine should follow a no-first-use declaration? To be meaningful, it would have to be accompanied by several changes. Concerning military doctrine, a no-first-use policy should be coupled with a renunciation of war-fighting doctrines, counterforce doctrines and doctrines of limited nuclear war. The removal of short-range tactical nuclear weapons from forward areas is an obvious first step. This could be followed by the creation of a complete nuclear-free zone in Europe. Obviously, a balance of conventional forces would then become even more important. Many analysts contend that a no-first-use declaration by the United States would require a significant increase in NATO's conventional capability. On the other hand, any such build-up by NATO could be matched by the WTO, leaving relative strengths unchanged. Another option would be to negotiate a reduction in the WTO's conventional capability until a balance is reached.

A no-first-use policy could contribute significantly to reduced tension. It could be a motivating force behind a restructuring of military forces and doctrine. It could lead to further reduction of nuclear armaments on both sides. It could contribute to improved U.S.-Soviet relations by enhancing stability. Finally, in the view of American leaders like Robert McNamara and George Kennan it offers "new hope to everyone in every country whose life is shadowed by the hideous possibility of a third great twentieth-century conflict in Europe—conventional or nuclear."[18]

Force Restructuring

Force restructuring is an approach that seeks agreements to change certain weapons on each side.[19] The changes may be in number and/or kind. This approach generally makes use of incremental agreements (small, specific, limited steps) rather than comprehensive agreements. Several agreements made separately can have a combined effect equal to that of more comprehensive agreements. The important thing for us to remember is that such agreements should implement a gradual shift away from a dependence on nuclear weapons.

A beginning point could be a focus on counterforce, or first-strike, weapons. For example, the United States might propose, as it has in the past, to eliminate the MX missile if the Soviet Union eliminated some portion of its MIRVed ICBM force. (Both weapons have the ability to hit multiple targets with a single rocket booster.) Or, as the Soviet Union proposed, the construction and deployment of large ballistic-missile submarines could be stopped on both sides.

Star Wars

Attempts to restructure our forces away from a reliance on counterforce capability should also include a condemnation of nuclear weapons in space. Admittedly, this is an ambitious proposal from the American point of view since the Reagan Administration has placed such heavy emphasis on its Strategic Defense Initiative (SDI—popularly called Star Wars). But extending nuclear weapons to space is a dangerous and destabilizing move. Not only is it a way to bolster nuclear war-fighting capabilities; it is also costly and would most likely thwart other attempts to reach arms-control agreements with the Soviet Union.

In his address to the nation on March 23, 1983, President Reagan issued his call for SDI: "I call upon the scientific community in our country, those who gave us nuclear weapons, to turn their great talents now to the cause of mankind and world peace, to give us the means of rendering these nuclear weapons impotent and obsolete."[20] With these words, President Reagan launched SDI with a strong appeal to moral sentiment. Now, he claimed, we could direct our energies to building defensive capability rather than offensive weapons. The Administration has continually argued that the only purpose of SDI is to defend the U.S. population against the threat of a Soviet attack. The argument put forth by most advocates of SDI is that even if the system is not leakproof, it would still serve to negate the Soviet first-strike option. Is SDI merely a defensive weapon?

The answer clearly is no. It is dishonest to ignore the offensive capabilities of SDI. U.S. space weapons *could* be used directly against Soviet satellites or other ground targets. The Soviets would have only our promise not to use SDI that way. The greatest fear from the Soviet point of view is the possibility that SDI could become a back-up system for a U.S. first strike. This fear seems all the more plausible considering the existence of U.S. war-fighting strategies and capability. It is also interesting to note that the Reagan Administration has testified on several occasions that it would view a Soviet counterpart to SDI in exactly this light. In fact, in his speech announcing SDI, Reagan also said, "If paired with offensive systems, [defensive systems such as SDI] can be viewed as fostering an aggressive policy."[21]

These questions were dealt with in the early 1970s when the superpowers considered the pursuit of antiballistic missile (ABM) programs. The conclusion reached then, which culminated in the ABM Treaty of 1972, was that ABM deployment was futile, destabilizing and costly.[22] It was viewed as futile because offensive weapons would win out in a competition with defensive weapons, especially against populations and urban areas. It was seen as destabilizing because the arms race would accelerate as both sides developed and deployed not only competing ABM systems but also offsetting systems to overpower, evade or attack the opponent's ABM. Many analysts believe these conclusions to be just as applicable today as they were in the early 1970s. Therefore, they expect that SDI will be seen in Moscow as "imposing a requirement for the most energetic reinforcement of all forms of Soviet nuclear capabilities—offensive, defensive, and counter-defensive."[23]

A final reason to oppose Star Wars is that it is likely to derail other arms-control efforts. The Reagan Administration contends, to the contrary, that SDI has served to bring the Soviets back to Geneva. This may be partly true, but, as noted by McGeorge Bundy, "The Soviet purpose in Geneva is to attack Star Wars, not negotiate any agreement which makes its objective legitimate."[24] Time and again, the Soviets have voiced their position that negotiations are contingent on an agreement not to extend the nuclear arms race into space. It is in our interest, then, to restructure our forces away from counterforce weapons and programs such as SDI as part of our scheme to negotiate a framework whereby reductions in nuclear weapons can result.

Freezes

Bilateral, Verifiable Nuclear Freeze. In contrast to the incremental approach described above, the nuclear-freeze proposal is comprehensive in nature. It calls for a bilateral, mutual, verifiable freeze on all further testing, production and deployment of nuclear weapons and of missiles and new aircraft designed primarily to deliver nuclear weapons. This comprehensiveness is the source of much criticism which centers on problems of negotiability. Comprehensive agreements take a long time to negotiate and may be unable to keep up with technological innovation. Moreover, some important agreements may not be ratified if parts of them are deemed unfavorable by either side. On the other hand, the United States and USSR have become familiar with this comprehensive approach through the SALT process, and it is one the Soviets seem to accept. Furthermore, comprehensive agreements have wide political appeal. The freeze movement, in particular, has been highly successful in mobilizing public opinion and putting political pressure on lawmakers. Senator Patrick Leahy (D-Vermont) describes the political effect of the freeze movement as follows:

> Whatever one might think about the arms control value of these new ideas, the very fact that some members of Congress feel compelled to seek an arms control framework for strategic modernization—and that the President finds it necessary to respond positively—is a substantial triumph for the nuclear freeze movement. Besides educating millions of Americans to the character and dangers of the arms race, it has made arms control efforts indispensable in an otherwise hostile administration.[25]

In spite of the difficulties, the freeze proposal has great merit. It would avoid further nuclear war-fighting developments (especially those in space) and make the renunciation of nuclear weapons more politically feasible. It would also inhibit the spread of nuclear arms by helping the United States and USSR meet their obligation under the 1968 Non-Proliferation Treaty (NPT) which pledges its signers to "pursue negotiations in good faith on effective measures relating to the cessation of the nuclear arms race at an early date."[26] Finally, the freeze would have obvious and significant economic benefits.

The real challenge comes in working through the problems of negotiability. Some freeze proponents argue that the most sensible approach is to begin with a partial freeze.[27] For example, it might be possible to freeze the most destabilizing weapons first, followed by less dangerous weapons. Other specific steps could also be considered: no further MIRVing (adding multiple warheads to a single missile) of existing weapons; freezing the number of land- and sea-based launch tubes for nuclear missiles; halting the production of fissionable material for weapons purposes; and suspending underground nuclear tests while working to negotiate a comprehensive test ban. Although our ultimate goal should remain a freeze on all nuclear weapons' technology and development as soon as possible, a less-than-total freeze (as a starting point) might be easier to negotiate. Hopefully progress in a partial freeze would encourage both sides to continue working for more comprehensive measures.

Comprehensive Test Ban. Some experts believe a comprehensive test ban (CTB) on the testing of nuclear weapons is "the most significant and achievable arms control measure at this time."[28] The goal of a CTB is threefold: to slow the momentum of the arms race; to preclude the development of new nuclear weapons; and to demonstrate the restraint of the superpowers in accord with the Non-Proliferation Treaty.

Test ban talks have long been an element of East-West arms control efforts. In 1963, the United States and USSR negotiated and ratified the Partial Test Ban Treaty which bans nuclear weapons tests in the air, underwater and in outer space. In the 1970s, two more treaties were negotiated but were never ratified by the United States. These were the Threshold Test Ban Treaty (TTBT) of 1974 and the Peaceful Nuclear Explosions Treaty (PNET) of 1976. Both put further limits on the yield and nature of allowable nuclear tests.

Currently negotiations are stalled. In 1980, President Carter suspended negotiations for a CTB as part of his response to the Soviet invasion of Afghanistan. The Reagan Administration has formally refused further CTB negotiations on several occasions.[29] The basic rationale put forth by the Administration for testing is that the United States needs to keep all options open. It needs to have the choice of developing different and better nuclear weapons. Testing, of course, is necessary to certify new designs and assure the reliability of our current stockpile. Critics also cite verification as a problem. Are there adequate answers to these concerns?

It is true that a test ban would erode confidence in existing stockpiles and hamper the development of new weapons. But this is a positive development! It would inhibit nuclear war-fighting policies. Reduced confidence in the nuclear stockpile would discourage a first strike since counterforce weapons must be precise and reliable.

Concerning verification, much evidence indicates that current means are sufficient. Verification of nuclear tests is done by measuring shock waves throughout the earth. United States capability in this area is highly sophisticated and "most experts concur that a network of some 25 seismic listening stations within the Soviet Union, plus 15 or so surrounding it, and a similar network in and around the United States would provide high confidence verification."[30] The United States could also take some unilateral steps such as enhancing resources devoted to monitoring nuclear tests.

The time is ripe for making significant progress on a comprehensive test ban. The USSR unilaterally halted all nuclear explosions until December 31, 1985. Then, in their January 1986 proposal, the Soviets extended this moratorium for three more months. The United States should take advantage of Soviet willingness to halt nuclear weapons explosions and join them in negotiating a formal CTB. We could begin by ratifying the already-negotiated TTBT and PNET while working on a comprehensive ban. Alternately, negotiations could begin with an interim agreement which would restrict the number and yield of tests each year, gradually becoming tighter over a period of time. Extensive verification measures could also be worked out to build confidence and trust. This interim agreement could end after a certain period, culminating in a complete test ban.

Reductions
Reducing the number of nuclear weapons is one essential feature of genuine arms control. Equivalence at current high levels is simply not sufficient. Reductions must be an integral part of our efforts to move away from a reliance on nuclear weapons for our

nation's security.

Phased, bilateral, verifiable reductions worked out in concert with the other proposals already discussed would increase everyone's security. There are several methods for reducing stockpiles of nuclear weapons which should be explored. One method calls for a fifty per cent reduction in United States and Soviet strategic nuclear-delivery vehicles in each of three categories: land-based missiles, submarine-based missiles and heavy bombers. In general, it is a reduction affecting all forms of nuclear weapons in equal measure. Currently this proposal is receiving much attention because it is a major component of the Soviet's January 1986 proposal.[31] One problem with the fifty-per-cent formula for reductions is that the forces of the two sides differ so much that each side prefers reductions in different areas. The fifty-per-cent proposal does not provide for the trade-offs that are often vital to successful negotiations.

A form of reductions that does take into account the asymmetries in United States and USSR force structures is called Percentage Annual Reductions (PAR). According to a PAR, the United States and USSR would agree to dismantle a percentage of their strategic delivery vehicles each year, with each side having the freedom to choose which weapons would be destroyed in a given year. This scheme requires agreement only once on a single percentage number, thus simplifying negotiations. Linking the two powers by a reduction rate would mean, in effect, running the arms race in reverse. Other nations could easily join this process of reduction.

Biblical peacemakers should throw themselves into the struggle for the mutual and verifiable elimination of nuclear weapons. And we should not succumb to the despair that abandons this goal as unrealistic. James Skillen, of the Association for Public Justice, is right: "Realism about present conditions which make that goal seem dreamy and utopian should not be equated with a cynicism that closes us off to God's call to work for justice here and now."[32]

Independent Initiatives

This chapter has stressed the importance of building peace by reducing our dependence on nuclear weapons through mutual agreement and action over time. This chapter has not advocated a policy of unilateral disarmament. Many Christians in the just war tradition would argue that in the present state of United States-Soviet relations, "the one situation more dangerous and more fraught with injustice than a balance of terror is a monopoly of terror."[33] This does not mean, however, that no unilateral steps should be taken. To the contrary, a number of independent initiatives could reduce East-West tensions and help free the world from bondage to nuclear weapons and the risk of nuclear war.

By independent initiatives I mean limited steps that the United States could take for a defined period of time which would be made conditional on an appropriate response from the Soviet Union. If that response were not forthcoming, the United States would no longer be bound by the initiative. The Episcopal bishops have suggested several such initiatives that deserve careful consideration:

1. The US should halt the flight testing of antisatellite weapons.
2. The US should begin to destroy obsolete tactical nuclear weapons and invite international observers to witness the destruction.
3. The US should reduce the testing of the most threatening nuclear war-fighting instruments such as MIRVed land-based missiles.
4. The US should join the USSR in halting nuclear weapons explosions underground as a step towards negotiating a CTB.[34]

Independent initiatives involve risk-taking. But certain risks are required to achieve progress in United States-Soviet relations and arms control. When U. S. initiatives clearly demonstrate peaceful intentions, when they constitute deeds as well as words, and when they generate international support, they have a good chance of building peace by fostering confidence, trust and stability.[35]

Conclusion

The steps suggested in the preceding pages do not constitute a complete answer to the nuclear problem. My purpose has been to suggest a general direction for bilateral, mutual nuclear disarmament within the framework of the just war tradition. And I have restricted the discussion to the bipolar relationship between the United States and Soviet Union because, in spite of growing pluralism, "the world has remained bipolar at the higher levels of nuclear force."[36] This is not to deny a crucial role in nuclear disarmament to Canadians, Western Europeans or even New Zealanders and citizens of the Third World. People everywhere have indispensable roles to play if we are to escape the nuclear cloud.

Nor has this chapter explored the broader ramifications of peacemaking. The struggle for economic justice is inextricably intertwined with the current arms race. When one remembers that the world's military expenditures each year equal the total income of the poorest one-half of humanity, one recalls the intimate link between peace and justice.

Indeed, as the Catholic bishops so eloquently remind us, the nuclear question is part of one seamless garment. If human life is almost infinitely precious to God, then we must say no to both infanticide and death by starvation, both abortion and nuclear weapons. Working to eliminate nuclear weapons is only one part of a consistent pro-life agenda.

Part 5

COMPLETELY PRO-LIFE

Chapter 10

Toward a Comprehensive Vision

No one can be a racist and at the same time be prolife. No one can be a religious bigot and at the same time be prolife. No one in this land of immigrants can cavalierly build a wall on our own shores that categorically says "No more!" and still claim to be prolife.[1]
Bernard F. Law

biblically informed pro-life agenda seeks fullness of life in every area. We have seen that this means dealing with both abortion and economic injustice, both the family and the nuclear arms race. These four issues are certainly among the most pressing pro-life concerns of our time. But they are not the only significant problems.

Wherever society fosters brokenness rather than shalom, pro-life people will demand change. The list of issues on a comprehensive pro-life agenda is almost limitless. This chapter can only hope to point, very briefly, to four other related areas—tobacco, alcoholism, environmental destruction and racism. I make no attempt whatsoever to deal adequately with any of them. But even a hasty overview will illustrate the breadth of any pro-life agenda which is faithful to the biblical vision of life and shalom.

Smoking

The U.S. Surgeon General, Dr. C. Everett Koop, has called smoking the "most important public health issue of our time."[2] According to William Pollin, the director of the U.S. National Institute on Drug Abuse, 350,000 persons in the United States alone die prematurely each year because of cigarette smoking. In a ringing editorial in the *Journal of the American Medical Association,* Pollin pointed out that these deaths are "more than all other drug and alcohol abuse deaths combined, seven times more than all automobile fatalities per year, more than a hundred times all recorded deaths caused by AIDS, and more than all American military fatalities in World War I, World War II, and Vietnam put together."[3]

American deaths from cigarette smoking are only one part of the total tragedy. Another approximately 500,000 die prematurely in Europe each year from cigarettes.[4] Thanks in part to Western advertising and even U.S. government subsidy of tobacco sales, cigarette consumption increased 25% in Latin America and 33% in Africa in the decade ending in 1983.[5] Because of the delayed effects of smoking, Third World deaths from cigarettes are only now becoming massive. But they will increase rapidly in the next decade. The global death toll from cigarette smoking already runs in the tens of millions. And it escalates every year.

Tragically, most smokers want to stop. Studies show that 90% of all regular smokers in the United States have tried to quit.[6] But they are trapped. Judging by the number of people who cannot control their intake, nicotine from cigarettes is six to eight times as addictive as alcohol. Most smokers become enslaved while still in their teens.[7]

The social costs are enormous. The U.S. Department of Health and Human Services says that smoking costs the nation annually $13 billion in medical bills, $25 billion in low productivity and $3.8 billion in Medicaid and Medicare expenditures.[8] It has been estimated that each employee who smokes costs his or her employer $1,000 annually.[9]

To add injury to insult, the U.S. taxpayer has subsidized the slaughter. Tobacco subsidies over half a century have cost taxpayers at least $700 million. We have also financed millions of dollars of agricultural research in tobacco.[10] And until quite recently we paid to send tobacco to Third World countries under our PL480 "Food for Peace" program. Jesse Helms, the great pro-life advocate in the Senate, has defended this policy because "historically these sales have developed new markets for American tobacco."[11]

Do pro-life Christians want to subsidize the export of death to the world's poor?

Moving effectively against this lucrative industry of death has been extremely difficult. The huge tobacco companies spend billions of dollars on advertising and contribute generously to political campaigns. Tobacco sales produced $8.7 billion in taxes for federal, state and local governments in the United States in 1983. So the companies have enormous economic and political clout. The huge sums spent in cigarette ads in newspapers and magazines intimidate even magazines like *Time* and *The New Republic* into killing stories on the dangers of smoking.[12] A short story in *Christianity Today* showed how Ronald Reagan reassured tobacco farmers in a letter in 1980: "I can guarantee that my own Cabinet members will be far too busy with substantive matters to waste their time proselytizing against the dangers of cigarette smoking."[13] Three hundred and fifty thousand deaths a year are not substantive?

What can be done? In 1985, the National Advisory Council on Drug Abuse urged President Reagan to propose legislation to eliminate all advertising and promotion of cigarettes in the United States. Since 1971, cigarette advertising has been banned on TV and radio. But the tobacco industry still advertises chewing tobacco and snuff—with great success among the young.[14]

We should insist on legislation that prohibits all tobacco promotion and advertising. Smoking in public places should be against the law. Citizens can encourage company policies that discourage smoking. And we should develop a mix of programs to encourage tobacco farmers to switch to other products. Most important, the church should set a good example!

Major campaigns by the church, the media and the government against this death-dealing industry must be an important element of any contemporary pro-life agenda.

Alcoholism

The United States has ten million alcoholics. Their personal tragedies entangle another thirty million family members, close friends and coworkers in a hell of crippling car accidents, fires, lost productivity and damaged health. That costs the nation, according to the Office of Technology Assessment, as much as $120 billion annually.[15]

That $120 billion loss includes far more than dollars. It means 100,000 alcohol-related deaths each year.[16] It means child abuse, spouse abuse, destroyed families and dissipated lives. This evil touches the lives of one of every five families.

Especially frightening is the devastation of our youth. Nineteen per cent (3.3 million) of our teen-agers between the ages of thirteen and seventeen have a drinking problem.[17] Drunk driving is the number one killer of American youth.

Drunk drivers kill 26,000 Americans every year. They cripple or seriously injure another one million. The economic loss from drunk driving alone is about $24 billion.[18]

It is no wonder that mothers are mad. MADD (Mothers Against Drunk Drivers) is one way to reduce this deadly toll. Christians concerned for life should support MADD's drive for tougher laws against drunk driving. Mandatory penalties, tougher sentences and more vigorous enforcement of the law all reduce the destruction of life.

But we need to go further. The alcohol merchants (largely huge multinational companies) annually spend $1 billion in the United states ($2 billion worldwide) to persuade us that more alcohol is the way to relaxation, happiness, success and status. And it works. Alcohol advertising jumped over 200% from 1970 to 1980. So did sales. Per capita U.S. consumption of alcohol increased 31.5% in that same period.[19]

Especially troubling is the way they target young people, heavy drinkers and nondrinkers (especially women). The companies deny all this, claiming that their advertising aims only to persuade people to switch brands (the cigarette companies repeat the same lie). But the careful research offered in *The Booze Merchants* proves otherwise.[20] These merchants of death advertise heavily in college newspapers and magazines for young, educated women. In fact, the brainwashing starts much earlier. The National Institute of Mental Health discovered that an American child sees an average of ten TV episodes with drinking every day.[21]

SMART is a new campaign to Stop Marketing of Alcohol on Radio and Television.[22] That is a good place to start. But we should demand more. We should prohibit by law all promotion and advertising of alcoholic beverages.

As in the case of smoking, indeed all the issues discussed in this book, the church needs to lead the way. Legislation is important but inadequate. In any case, it is possible only when society's basic values allow it. A pro-life church will say no vigorously to the values that produce death by alcohol.

Racism
Racism is alive and well in South Africa and south Philadelphia, India and Indiana. Racism, like sin, is not a white, male, middle-class phenomena. Whether in Sri Lanka or Soweto, it maims and kills millions.

The Hindu caste system which now subjects 150 million low-caste Indians to incredible degradation and destruction has its origins in Aryan prejudice against people of a different, darker race.[23] Daily headlines call our attention to the unequal education, poverty and death that result from South Africa's white-imposed system of apartheid. (For an extensive treatment of South Africa by experts of many different perspectives, see the April-June 1986 issue of _Transformation_.)

For Americans the first priority must be the stubborn persistence of racism in a nation that would like to think that the civil-rights movement ended centuries of racial oppression. My own city proves otherwise. In late 1985 and early 1986, Philadelphians claimed to be shocked by front-page stories about black and interracial families who moved into all-white neighborhoods only to be driven out by threats, mobs and arsonists. Sadly that is still a reality for many black Americans.

Prejudice has stubborn roots. In early May, 1985, a pollster explained to the leaders of the Democratic Party gathered in Chicago that his polling indicated that white voters were abandoning the Democratic Party largely for one reason. He found that "the party's recent defectors, almost all of whom are white, are leaving party ranks largely because they feel that federal domestic programs . . . stacked the deck in favor of blacks."[24]

In spite of some important affirmative-action programs and voting-rights laws, that was hardly the case. As the chart on page 120 of chapter six shows, blacks earn significantly less than do whites at every job level.[25] The typical black family headed by a person with a high-school education earns only 61% of what a typical white family headed by a person with the same education earns.[26] From 1980-1984 the average black two-parent family with one parent working lost $2,000 in income. In those years, poverty among blacks increased twice as fast as it did among whites.[27]

Obviously the causes of black poverty are complex. It would be simplistic nonsense to blame it all on white racism. But racism is surely one cause. Pro-life Christians will say no to poverty and death by racial prejudice.

Environmental Destruction
Created a little lower than the angels and destined for life eternal

in the presence of the living God, persons soar above their earthly environment. Created out of dust and condemned to return to it, persons remain fundamentally interrelated with the earth. The Author of life chose to make humanity dependent on the rocks and rivers, soil and trees of his good creation.

Foolishly, modern civilization recklessly devastates the natural environment on which life depends. The United States loses 3 million acres of agricultural land each year. Annually, erosion carries away 6.4 billion tons of topsoil—enough to cover all crop land in Maine, New Hampshire, Vermont, Massachusetts, Connecticut, Rhode Island, New York, New Jersey, Pennsylvania, Delaware, Maryland, Alabama, California and Florida with an inch of dirt. Since we began farming in North America, one-third of all our topsoil has been lost forever.[28]

Every day, erosion and development remove enough productive land to feed 260,000 people for a year.[29] In a world of hunger and starvation, that is a pro-life issue.

Increasingly the world's limited supply of water is threatened. In the United States, a spot check by the Environmental Protection Agency of more than 8,000 hazardous-waste disposal sites revealed that three-quarters were merely holes in the ground. Once underground reservoirs are contaminated, they are ruined indefinitely. Salinization, waterlogging and alkalinization have already damaged half of the world's irrigated land.[30]

Acid rain destroys rivers, lakes and forests in North America, Europe and the Soviet Union. Even more serious, some studies indicate that increasing use of fossil fuels will double the carbon dioxide in the atmosphere and produce a warming trend that will melt the polar ice caps and cause a catastrophic rise in sea-levels.[31]

Pessimistic warnings of catastrophic threats have made us numb and callous. Undoubtedly some predictions have been exaggerated and some alleged threats unfounded. That a basic problem exists, however, is beyond debate. And it is a life-and-death issue.

Fortunately there are solutions, if we are willing to pay the cost.

We could make it a high priority to move from hard energy to soft energy. The current path of hard energy places primary emphasis on fossil fuels that pollute and on nuclear energy that creates undisposable hazardous wastes.[32] The soft energy route would stress renewable natural resources such as sun, wind and water. A "Solar Sweden Study" reported that "by 2015 Sweden could shift entirely to solar energy without prohibitive costs and without major changes in lifestyle."[33] A study for the U.S. Department of Energy found similarly that by 2025 California could largely exist on local renewable energy sources.[34]

We can correct environmental pollution if we act now. But it will take vigorous political action by people who know that returning to the task of respectful stewardship of God's good garden is a pro-life issue.

The four vast areas hinted at in this chapter do not exhaust the list of significant pro-life concerns.[35] A comprehensive vision includes biotechnology, euthanasia, capital punishment and much more. As the biblical vision of life and shalom shapes our values, we will lovingly call every area of life back to the wholeness God desires.

Chapter 11

A Historic Opportunity

N ever in the twentieth century have theologically conservative Christians enjoyed such favorable prospects for shaping American public life. We have repented of and abandoned an earlier neglect or even disdain for politics. A host of new organizations, periodicals and educational institutions produce increasingly sophisticated analyses of social issues. The larger society, including the media and the political leadership, increasingly accept biblical Christians as important, respected partners in the shaping of public life. If we are wise and faithful, we can impact our nation and the world in a crucial way in the last fifteen years of this millennium.

Success, however, is not guaranteed. It would be easy to squander this historic opportunity. In order not to'do that, we need biblical balance at every point. In the preceding chapters we have seen that biblical balance involves a political agenda devoted to all the issues the Bible says God is interested in. This balance must be manifested in four other areas as well: in both evangelism and social responsibility; in both prayer and action; in an emphasis on both the church as Jesus' new community and the transformation of the larger society; and in showing both truth and love in debate. Balance in these four areas is essential if we are to maximize today's unique opportunity.

We need more evangelism, not less, in the next decades. As we throw ourselves intensely into the struggle to make public life a little more just, free and peaceful, we dare not forget that even the most far-reaching political change will have only limited success. Restructuring society cannot get to the root of selfish personalities. Only redeeming grace can do that. Therefore, we must make sure that our zeal for evangelism does not lag because of increased attention to societal change.

That does not mean that structural change is irrelevant. Enabling black Americans to vote, poor folk to find jobs, babies to enjoy life, and the next generation to face fewer military weapons are all significant. Biblical people will work hard for those things. But even if we succeed beyond our wildest dreams, we will not produce utopia. Politicians will still sometimes be corrupt and people will still be selfish. Everyone will still need the forgiveness and sanctification that Christ alone can give. Only if we maintain a biblical balance between evangelism and social concern and only if we reject the liberal illusion that mere societal engineering can create new persons, will we have maximum impact on the social order.

Prayer is also fundamental. If we think that we can transform the social order merely by sophisticated techniques, then we will fail. If we proudly trust in our new mastery of direct mail, advanced polling techniques and manipulation of the media, we underestimate and misunderstand the enemy. It is still true that we fight not against flesh and blood but against demonic principalities and powers. Our ultimate enemy is the Satanic One who fights with total abandon to defile and destroy God's good creation. Only prayer and a radical dependence on the Holy Spirit are powerful enough for battle with such a foe.

To insist that the enemy is Satan is not to say that persons who disagree with our political analysis are in league with the devil (or

Moscow). That kind of arrogance is both counterproductive and unchristian. Rather, it is to say that we enter the political arena knowing that societal problems result not just from selfish persons but also from Satan's deadly forays into the good creation. Knowing that his influence is everywhere (not least in our own limited insight and partial efforts), we will plead humbly for divine help. We will also refuse to equate our political wisdom with the kingdom of God.

Prayer therefore will be central to faithful Christians' political activity. That was certainly true in the past. Historians tell us that Wilberforce and his band of antislavery crusaders immersed their political strategizing and lobbying in daily three-hour sessions of intercessory prayer.[1] Charles Finney was both the Billy Graham of the midnineteenth century and a leading crusader against slavery. Finney insisted that long hours of prayer were central to his work.[2] Andrew Murray has said that in prayer we hold the hand that holds the destiny of the universe. In fact, Murray dared to say that by prayer we "determine the history of this earth."[3]

That does not mean that we neglect action. The most sophisticated political activity is essential. But we must combine that political expertise with a pervasive conviction that finally the struggle belongs to God and we prevail not by might nor by power but by prayerful trust in the Sovereign of history.

Failure to distinguish clearly between church and nation would also weaken or destroy effective Christian impact on the social order. The church is Jesus' new messianic community living by the standards of Jesus' dawning kingdom. Necessarily, therefore, the church is always a loving critic of the status quo, conserving all that is good and challenging all that is evil. By grace it is now possible for the church to model these new values in a way that the larger society cannot. In the church we experience the liberating power of forgiveness, the transforming dynamic of the sanctifying Spirit, and the empowering support of other sisters and brothers. The church therefore should offer to a fallen world a little picture now of what heaven will be like. The church should be far ahead of the rest of society in overcoming the brokenness of fallen creation.

It is only as we understand and incarnate this distinction between Christ's new redeemed community and the fallen social order that we can successfully impact society. Too often Christians fail to see the sharp dichotomy between church and nation, and between the kingdom's values and society's values. As a result, Christians are often carbon copies of the world. When that happens, their political impact (no matter how massive) is largely useless because it merely reinforces the evil of the status quo. Only if Christians understand clearly the difference between biblical values and prevailing social norms can they creatively move society in the direction of God's shalom.

Similarly, it is only as the church truly models the values it proclaims that its political activity has integrity. Too often Christian leaders ask Washington to legislate what their parishioners refuse to live. That is a farce. If I am not willing to allow the Holy Spirit to heal the brokenness in my relationship with my wife, I lack integrity when I advise my senator on international reconciliation. If our local congregations are not beginning to model a biblical concern for the poor, weak and marginalized, then it is hypocritical to summon the president to costly political decisions that place justice for the poor above short-term political advantage. On the other hand, living communities of Christians whose common life demonstrates the possibility of reconciled, just relationships between black and white, rich and poor, male and female, have a profound social impact.

Here, too, of course, the church as new community is no substitute for vigorous political engagement. Sophisticated, patient, political activity is imperative. But it is only as the church understands how profoundly Jesus' values challenge current norms and as it incarnates those biblical norms, that its vigorous political involvement will have integrity and power.

Finally, we need both truth and love, both vigor and respect, in political debate. Too often recent Christian political involvement has been identified with smear campaigns of distortion and hate. Name-calling, slanderous stereotyping and one-sided distortions of opponents' positions are on the increase. Unless we develop a new covenant of civility and integrity in debate, we may provoke hostility, lose credibility or self-destruct in ferocious fratricide.

Biblical Christians must enter the political arena with a deep respect for the religious and political pluralism of our society. Everyone, including secular humanists, have a right to life, liberty and the pursuit of their political agenda. Carefully demonstrating and vigorously opposing the destructive effects of misguided views on the family or the sanctity of human life are not only permissible, but necessary. But name-calling and funding political hate campaigns is not. If Christian political involvement does not respect the views of others in our pluralistic society, we will provoke a devastating secular counterattack.

A covenant of fair debate within the Christian community is also urgent. There is enormous political disagreement about the issues discussed in this book, even among sincere Bible-believing Christians. The only way to settle those disagreements is by reading our Bibles and newspapers together in open, respectful dialog. Name-calling and stereotyping do not foster that open exchange. I disagree intensely with Jerry Falwell's views on the nuclear arms race. But I believe he desires peace in the world as much as I do. It is valid for me to argue that the nuclear build-up he endorses will increase the danger of nuclear war. But it would be immoral name-calling to refer to him as a warmonger. Conversely, it is quite proper for him to charge that my support of a bilateral, verifiable nuclear freeze increases the danger of nuclear war. But it would be slander to call me a Marxist.

One significant Christian contribution to political life ought to be a demonstration of integrity and fairness in debate. We can resolve to forgo distortion, half-truth, slander, name-calling and hate tactics. We can demonstrate that one criterion of honest debate is stating an opponent's views in such a way that he or she says, "Yes, that is what I mean."

Both truth and love must characterize Christian political debate. That does not preclude forthright condemnation of error. The debate should flow fast but not furious, vigorous but not vicious. If we fail to guarantee that, our political impact in the coming years will fall far short of its potential.[4]

If we debate fairly, live what we preach, distinguish between church and nation, pray as much as we act, retain our passion for evangelism and adopt a truly biblical political agenda, we can profoundly shape history at the end of the twentieth century.

What William Wilberforce accomplished in late eighteenth- and early nineteenth-century Britain may be possible again today. Praying and politicking, Wilberforce led the grand crusade against the slave trade and then slavery for thirty long years. Through faithful participation as a member of Parliament, he ended a terrible violation of the sanctity of human life. Through Wilberforce, biblical faith significantly changed the British Empire.

Comparable or even greater changes are necessary if a consistent, biblically informed pro-life agenda is to prevail in the modern world. I believe the Sovereign of history will do again today what he did in the time of Wilberforce if his people will adopt a biblical agenda and strategy.

Even then, of course, the results will be limited. Wilberforce changed, but did not perfect, his society. Neither will we. But even modest success is worth heroic effort. If we can reduce by a few tens of millions those who die of abortion and starvation; if we can help a few tens of millions of families enjoy happier homes and more secure futures; if we can reduce the pollution of our streams and lungs; if we can bequeath to our children a world less threatened by nuclear holocaust, that will be enough. Even such imperfect signs of coming shalom will be sufficient to confirm the belief that the Author of life is still the Lord of politics.

Appendix A

Chicago Declaration of Evangelical Social Concern

As evangelical Christians committed to the Lord Jesus Christ and the full authority of the Word of God, we affirm that God lays total claim upon the lives of his people. We cannot, therefore, separate our lives from the situation in which God has placed us in the United States and the world.

We confess that we have not acknowledged the complete claim of God on our lives.

We acknowledge that God requires love. But we have not demonstrated the love of God to those suffering social abuses.

We acknowledge that God requires justice. But we have not proclaimed or demonstrated his justice to an unjust American society. Although the Lord calls us to defend the social and economic rights of the poor and oppressed, we have mostly remained silent. We deplore the historic involvement of the church in America with racism and the conspicuous responsibility of the evangelical community for perpetuating the personal attitudes and institutional structures that have divided the body of Christ along color lines. Further, we have failed to condemn the exploitation of racism at home and abroad by our economic system.

We affirm that God abounds in mercy and that he forgives all who repent and turn from their sins. So we call our fellow evangelical Christians to demonstrate repentance in a Christian discipleship that confronts the social and political injustice of our nation.

We must attack the materialism of our culture and the maldistribution of the nation's wealth and services. We recognize that as a nation we play a crucial role in the imbalance and injustice of international trade and development. Before God and a billion hungry neighbors, we must rethink our values regarding our present standard of living and promote a more just acquisition and distribution of the world's resources.

We acknowledge our Christian responsibilities of citizenship. Therefore, we must challenge the misplaced trust of the nation in economic and military might—a proud trust that promotes a national pathology of war and violence which victimizes our neighbors at home and abroad. We must resist the temptation to make the nation and its institutions objects of near-religious loyalty.

We acknowledge that we have encouraged men to prideful domination and women to irresponsible passivity. So we call both men and women to mutual submission and active discipleship.

We proclaim no new gospel, but the Gospel of our Lord Jesus Christ who, through the power of the Holy Spirit, frees people from sin so that they might praise God through works of righteousness.

By this declaration, we endorse no political ideology or party, but call our nation's leaders and people to that righteousness which exalts a nation.

We make this declaration in the biblical hope that Christ is coming to consummate the Kingdom and we accept his claim on our total discipleship until he comes.

November 25, 1973
Chicago, Illinois

Appendix B

Here We Stand: A Reaffirmation of ESA's Commitments

The following statement was developed by the ESA Board of Directors during the summer of 1984. Its purpose is to clarify and reaffirm the beliefs and convictions upon which ESA is based.

I. As members of ESA we have only one goal and one source of authority. With all our heart, mind and strength, we seek to glorify Jesus Christ, the Risen Lord, in obedience to the Scriptures.

II. Rejecting ideologies of left and right, we prayerfully seek to apply biblical principles to the desperate problems of modern society. This means that we cannot choose issues or project policies and programs on the basis of popular appeal or current interest. Evangelical endeavors to change public life must reflect the whole range of biblical concerns and emphases. We therefore welcome the challenges to and criticisms of our activities made by fellow-believers who, like ourselves, accept the Old and New Testaments as the only infallible rule of faith and practice.

III. With sadness we observe how easy it is for Christian social movements to lose their biblical foundations. We therefore affirm our unchanged conviction that historic Christian orthodoxy, and it alone, can provide a solid foundation for enduring social reform.

IV. Recognizing creation as the gift of the triune God, who made persons in His own image, we accept His mandate to be faithful stewards of the earth and to respect the sacredness of human life. We acknowledge that our own lifestyles must demonstrate our commitment through personal righteousness and stewardship of our time, talent and resources for the advancement of God's Kingdom.

V. Realizing that because of the Fall human beings are in bondage to sin, we repudiate secular plans to transform society through mere structural change and environmental improvement. Humanity's proud rebellion against God expresses environmental improvement. Humanity's proud rebellion against God expresses itself in both personal and social sin. Aware, then, that the restraining hand of government can reduce the ways sin becomes embedded in socio-economic systems, we dedicate ourselves to work for policies that promote liberty, justice and peace.

We know, however, that changing structures can never create new individuals as Marxists and humanists claim. Only personal conversion and the transforming power of the Spirit can release us from the bondage of selfishness rooted in the heart.

VI. We therefore reaffirm our belief in the centrality of evangelism. We seek to avoid those mistakes of the earlier Christian social movements that neglected or abandoned evangelistic concern. Enthusiastically we support the evangelistic mission of sister organizations, knowing that without them our task is impossible and incomplete. We rejoice in biblical evangelism which calls for repentance from all sin, both personal and social. Only an evangelism which summons people to costly discipleship can create new persons and build a Christocentric community capable of challenging materialism, racism, militarism and totalitarianism. We thank God for redemptive grace and saving faith which liberate through the free pardon of sin, and empower love of neighbor that works for peace and justice.

VII. While evangelism is not social action and salvation is not social justice, these are intimately and inseparably related. So we pray for a mighty outpouring of the Holy Spirit in our day to convert sinners, revive believers and show all Christians that biblical faith must motivate a passionate commitment to justice, peace and liberty.

VIII. Knowing that spiritual revival and social reformation cannot take place except through God's sovereign initiative and enablement, we dedicate ourselves to renewed intercession and dependence on the Holy Spirit. We believe that prayer should be as central to our social action as it is to evangelistic campaigns. Therefore we seek to immerse political and economic concerns in prayer, entreating the Spirit's supernatural power and transforming presence.

IX. Jesus came preaching, healing and feeding. He demonstrated the Good News that the Kingdom of God has truly invaded human history. We therefore reject the escapism that abandons history to Satan's pseudo-lordship and anticipates no amelioration of evil until our Lord's return. We seek here and now to follow the way of Christ by the power of the Holy Spirit. Yet knowing that Christ's Kingdom will not be fully present before His second coming, we repudiate the utopianism which expects unlimited progress in human history. Therefore, even as we strive for the genuine but limited progress that is possible now, we look eagerly for the perfection that will come at Christ's return. For His bodily resurrection assures us that in God's good time the creation itself will be freed from its bondage to decay and death.

X. In light of this confession, we as members of Evangelicals for Social Action continue our commitment to a consistent prolife agenda. We oppose governments of the left and right which violate human rights, ignore religious and political freedoms, or neglect the needs of the poor. We oppose abortion on demand which destroy's millions of lives each year. We oppose, as well, the escalating arms race which increasingly threatens to annihilate millions of human beings made in God's image. We support public policies which protect and preserve the environment. We support all strategies and agencies that strengthen the family and support the view that marriage is a life-long covenant between one man and one woman. We seek to be informed about and responsive to human suffering that results from oppressive and unjust economic systems. We seek an end to institutionalized racism and discrimination based on ethnicity, gender, age or physical ability. We seek to preserve and extend democratic systems and the freedoms upon which democracies are based.

XI. We confess, too, that applying biblical teaching to the complex problems of contemporary life is difficult. So we undertake this task with humility, realizing that all human wisdom is limited. But to shrink from this task would be a denial of the Lordship of Christ over all creation and history. Hence we proceed with resolute vigor, grateful when we falter for our Lord's forgiveness and the correction administered through fellow believers. We trust that God will use our imperfect efforts to bring ourselves, our nation and our world into closer alignment with God's justice, peace and liberty.

Notes

Chapter 1: Fullness of Life

[1]Michael J. Gorman, *Abortion and the Early Church* (Downers Grove: InterVarsity Press, 1982), p. 90.

[2]From a speech entitled "A Consistent Ethic of Life: Continuing the Dialogue," given at St. Louis University, 11 Mar. 1984, published in Joseph Bernardin, *The Seamless Garment* (Kansas City: National Catholic Reporter, 1984), p. 10.

[3]*Religious News Service,* 1 Aug. 1984, p. 7.

[4]See also Acts 3:15; 17:25; Genesis 1—2.

[5]See Ronald J. Sider, "Green Politics: Biblical or Buddhist?" *SCP Newsletter* 11, no. 3 (Fall 1985):7-11.

[6]Peter Singer, *Animal Liberation* (New York: New York Review Book, 1975), p. 21.

[7]See Loren Wilkinson, ed., *Earth Keeping: Christian Stewardship of Natural Resources* (Grand Rapids: Eerdmans, 1980).

[8]God is the source of *shalom* (Num 6:26; 1 Kings 2:33; Ps 29:11; 122:69; 147:14; Is 9:6-7; 45:7; 48:18; Jer 33:6). *Shalom* includes material prosperity (Ex 4:18; 2 Chron 34:28; Ps 37:11; Is 38:1; Hag 2:9; Zech 8:12), physical security and freedom from anxiety (Judg 6:23; 18:6; 1 Sam 1:17), and the absence of warfare (Deut 2:26; Josh 9:15; Judg 21:13; 1 Sam 7:14; 1 Kings 4:24; Ps 120:7; Jer 6:14).

[9]Leviticus 26:7ff. shows that *shalom* in this text is not incompatible with Israel slaying her neighbors. But later Old Testament material shows that the fullness of *shalom* will mean an end to the sword for all people (for example, see Is 2:1-4; Mic 4:1ff.).

[10]See the same connection in Romans 8:6.

[11]For a fuller discussion of the use of paradigms, see Christopher J. H. Wright, "The Use of the Bible in Social Ethics," *Transformation,* Jan.-Mar. 1984, espe-

cially pp. 16-18; and Ronald J. Sider, "An Evangelical Vision for Public Policy," *Transformation*, July-Sept. 1985, p. 4.

[12]See Wright, "Use of the Bible," pp. 16-17.

[13]*Christianity Today*, 4 Sept. 1981, p. 27.

[14]*Newsweek*, 21 Sept. 1981, p. 17—italics added.

[15]Nat Hentoff, "The Awful Privacy of Baby Doe," *Atlantic Monthly*, Jan. 1985, pp. 59-62; and "How Can the Left Be Against Life?" *Village Voice*, 16 July 1985, pp. 18, 20.

[16]*Sojourners*, Nov. 1980.

[17]See *Christianity Today*, 12 July 1985, pp. 40, 42.

[18]See especially the appendixes in this book and the ESA tract, "Can My Vote Be Biblical?" as well as regular items in the monthly ESA *Update* available from Evangelicals for Social Action, Box 76560, Washington, D.C. 20013.

[19]For information, write to JustLife, P.O. Box 15263, Washington, D.C. 20003 or call 202-543-9530. See also *Christianity Today*, 13 June 1986, pp. 36-37.

[20]Lowell O. Erdahl, *Pro-Life/Pro-Peace* (Minneapolis: Augsburg, 1986). See also Bernard Haring, *The Healing Power of Peace and Non-Violence* (New York: Paulist, 1986).

[21]National Conference of Catholic Bishops, *The Challenge of Peace: God's Promise and Our Response* (Boston: St. Paul Editions, 1983), especially sections 284-89 on pp. 88-89.

[22]Bernardin, *Seamless Garment*.

Chapter 2: Biblical Faith and the Unborn

[1]Peter Singer, "Sanctity of Life or Quality of Life?" *Pediatrics* 72, no. 1 (July 1983):129.

[2]John T. Noonan, Jr., "Raw Judicial Power," *National Review*, 2 Mar. 1973, p. 261.

[3]Kenneth Kantzer, "The Origin of the Soul as Related to the Abortion Question," in Walter O. Spitzer and Carlyle L. Saylor, *Birth Control and the Christian* (Wheaton: Tyndale, 1969), p. 553.

[4]Spitzer and Saylor, *Birth Control and the Christian*, p. xxv.

[5]Ibid., p. xxvi.

[6]For a recent evangelical defense of abortion in very limited situations, see D. Gareth Jones, *Brave New People* (Grand Rapids: Eerdmans, 1985), chap. 7. See also Lewis Penhall Bird, "Dilemmas in Biomedical Ethics," Carl F. H. Henry, ed., *Horizons of Science* (New York: Harper and Row, 1978), pp. 139ff.

[7]Carl F. H. Henry, *The Christian Mindset in a Secular Society* (Portland: Multnomah, 1984), p. 103.

[8]Curt Young, *The Least of These* (Chicago: Moody, 1983) p. 105; documentation in nn. 8-10.

[9]Maggie Scarf, "The Fetus as Guinea Pig," *New York Times Magazine* 19 (Oct. 1975):92.

[10]Val Dorgan, "Foetuses Experiments," *Cork Examiner*, 25 Aug. 1983.

[11]Hentoff, "The Awful Privacy of Baby Doe," p. 55. See also his "How Can the Left Be Against List?" *The Village Voice,* 16 July 1985, pp. 18, 20.

[12]See too the report of a similar situation in Oklahoma in "Early Management and Decision Making for the Treatment of Myelomeningocele," *Pediatrics,* Oct. 1983.

[13]See its defense by Joseph Fletcher, *Morals and Medicine* (Princeton, N.J.: Princeton University Press, 1954), pp. 172- 210.

[14]Young, *Least of These,* pp. 132-33.

[15]*Denver Post,* 28 Mar. 1984.

[16]Quoted in Hentoff, "The Awful Privacy of Baby Doe," p. 55.

[17]"American Abortion Dilemma," *Newsweek,* 14 Jan. 1985, p. 29.

[18]Quoted in ibid.

[19]*Scientific American,* June 1980, p. 42.

[20]Ibid. See also the studies by Arthur Shastak of Drexel University mentioned in Young, *Least of These,* pp. 65-66.

[21]See the references in Young, *Least of These,* p. 64, nn. 19-25.

[22]An anonymous article entitled, "An Apology to a Little Boy I Won't Ever See," *Providence Evening Bulletin,* 23 Apr. 1980. Women Exploited by Abortion (12310 Flamingo Lane, Bowie, MD 20715) is an organization dealing honestly with this trauma.

[23]Young, *Least of These,* p. 65.

[24]Philip G. Ney, "A Consideration of Abortion Survivors," *Child Psychiatry and Human Development* 13, no. 3 (Spring 1983):170. See similar findings in Anita H. and Eugene C. Weiner, "The Aborted Sibling Factor," *Clinical Social Work Journal* 12, no. 3 (Fall 1984):209-15.

[25]Ney, "Abortion Survivors," p. 172.

[26]Stanley Hauerwas, *A Community of Character* (Notre Dame, Ind.: University of Notre Dame Press, 1981) p. 211.

[27]John T. Noonan, Jr., "An Almost Absolute Value in History," in John T. Noonan, ed., *The Morality of Abortion: Legal and Historical Perspectives* (Cambridge: Harvard University Press, 1970), pp. 1-59.

[28]See Beverly Wilding Harrison's fascinating revision of the historical material in *Our Right to Choose: Toward a New Ethic of Abortion* (Boston: Beacon Press, 1983), pp. 119-86.

[29]Gorman, *Abortion and the Early Church,* p. 81; see pp. 77-82 for an extended discussion of this point.

[30]Noonan, *Morality of Abortion,* pp. 1-59.

[31]*Newsweek,* 14 Jan 1985, p. 29.

[32]Kristin Luker, *Abortion and the Politics of Motherhood* (Berkeley: University of California Press, 1984), pp. 194-97.

[33]See, for example, *Abortion and the Poor: Private Morality, Public Responsibility* (New York: The Alan Guttmacher Institute, 1979), p. 32.

[34]Norman B. Bendroth, "Abortion and the Third Way of the Kingdom," Richard

Cizik, ed., *The High Cost of Indifference* (Ventura: Regal Books, 1983), p. 58. See the same kind of argument exposed in Hentoff, "The Awful Privacy of Baby Doe," p. 58.
[35]Quoted in James T. Burtchaell, *Rachel Weeping* (San Francisco: Harper and Row, 1984), p. 150.
[36]Linda Bird Francke, *The Ambivalence of Abortion* (New York: Random House, 1978).
[37]Harrison, *Our Right to Choose*, p. 163. See p. 266, n. 23 for the research of Judith Blake. Her data comes from the sixties and early seventies. See also the discussion of male pressure in *Sojourners*, Nov. 1980, pp. 4-8.
[38]Harrison, *Our Right to Choose*, p. 195.
[39]*National Catholic Reporter*, 22 Feb. 1985, p. 10—Dale's italics.
[40]Harrison, *Our Right to Choose*, p. 16.
[41]Ginny Earnest Soley, "To Preserve and Protect Life: A Christian Feminist Perspective on Abortion," *Sojourners*, Oct. 1986, pp. 34-37.
[42]"If value is something that only human beings confer, then the pro-choice point of view must ultimately prevail" (John Garvey, "Who Confers Value?" *Commonweal*, 9 Aug. 1985. p. 424).
[43]"Report of the Committee to Study the Matter of Abortion," in Minutes of the Thirty-Eighth General Assembly, The Orthodox Presbyterian Church (7401 Old York Road, Philadelphia, PA 19126), 24-29 May 1971, p. 146—their italics (hereafter cited as OPC Study [1971]). So similarly, John Jefferson Davis, *Abortion and the Christian* (Phillipsburg, N.J.: Presbyterian and Reformed, 1984), p. 61.
[44]OPC Study (1971), p. 146.
[45]Ibid., pp. 146-48.
[46]See, for instance, Bruce Waltke, "The Old Testament and Birth Control," *Christianity Today*, 8 Nov. 1968, p. 3 (Waltke has subsequently revised his position); and the many commentaries and translations mentioned in Jack Cottrell, "Abortion and the Mosaic Law," *Christianity Today*, 16 Mar. 1973, p. 7. Also Harrison, *Our Right to Choose*, pp. 68-69. Extra-biblical material from the Code of Hammurabi has influenced the RSV translation. Sections 209-14 discuss the penalty for striking a pregnant woman and assign a modest fine when a miscarriage results and a heavy fine when death to the mother occurs. See James Bennett Pritchard, *Ancient Near Eastern Texts Relating to the Old Testament*, 2nd ed. (Princeton, N.J.: Princeton University Press, 1955), p. 175.
[47]OPC Study (1971), p. 141—their italics.
[48]See the argument in Cottrell, "Abortion and the Mosaic Law," p. 8; the OPC Study (1971), pp. 142-43; and Davis, *Abortion and the Christian*, pp. 49-52; John Warwick Montgomery, *Slaughter of the Innocents* (Westchester, Ill.: Crossway Books, 1981), pp. 98-101; C. F. Deil and Franz Delitzsch, *Biblical Commentary on the Old Testament: The Pentateuch*, vol. 2, trans. James Martin (Grand Rapids: Eerdmans, n.d.), pp. 134-35; and the Jewish scholar, Umberto Cassuto, *Commen-*

tary on the Book of Exodus, trans. Israel Abrahams (Jerusalem: Magnes Press, the Hebrew University, 1967), p. 275.

[49]It should be noted, however, that the word *prematurely* in the NIV translation is not in the Hebrew text of Exodus 21:22. Both the NIV and the RSV are, to some extent, interpretations.

[50]See Oliver O'Donovan's discussion of the exception, namely, identical twins, in *The Christian and the Unborn Child,* 2nd ed. (Bramcote Notts: Grove Books, 1975), pp. 12-13.

[51]*California Medicine* 113, no. 3 (1979), quoted in Davis, *Abortion and the Christian,* p. 22.

[52]Gerhard von Rad, *Old Testament Theology,* vol. 1, trans. D. Stalker (New York: Harper and Row, 1962), p. 145. See the discussion in Davis, pp. 52-54.

[53]O'Donovan, *Christian and the Unborn Child,* p. 11.

[54]See O'Donovan's comment on this in ibid., p. 5. Albert Outler echoes this opinion: "if it is only *probable* that a fetus is a human being . . . then we would do better to recognize abortion as a moral evil in every case and thus, even when chosen, a tragic option of what has been judged to be the lesser of two real evils" ("The Beginning of Personhood," *Perkins School of Theology Journal* 68 (June 1971):32—*Outler's italics.*

[55]Paul Ramsey, "Abortion, a Review Article," *Thomist* 37 (1973):174ff.

[56]See Harrison's insistence that it is and ought to be a major method of birth control in, for example, *Right to Choose,* pp. 42, 162.

[57]See Davis, *Abortion and the Christian,* pp. 30-31 and studies cited in nn. 22-27.

[58]O'Donovan, *Christian and the Unborn Child,* p. 19.

[59]OPC Study (1971), p. 153.

[60]Ethel Waters with Charles Samuels, *His Eye Is on the Sparrow* (Garden City, N.Y.: Doubleday, 1951), pp. 3-4.

Chapter 3: Abortion and Public Policy

[1]Karl Barth, *Church Dogmatics,* vol. 3, pt. 4 (Edinburgh: T. and T. Clark, 1961), p. 419.

[2]Roe vs. Wade, 410 U.S. 113, 162.

[3]Douglas Badger, "Abortion:The Judeo-Christian Imperative," *Whose Values?* Carl Horn, ed. (Ann Arbor, Mich.: Servant, 1985), p. 82.

[4]Gov. Mario Cuomo in a speech delivered at the Department of Theology, Notre Dame University, Sept. 13, 1984, and reprinted in *Human Life Review* 11, nos. 1-2, p. 27.

[5]Ibid.

[6]In a narrow technical sense, to be sure, the labels have validity. If abortion is murder, then those who commit abortion are in a basic objective sense murderers. And if rapidly expanding the arms race increases the danger of war, then the people who do that are in a basic objective sense people who "stir up war." But this analysis ignores the moral intention of both persons. Pro-

choice people do not intend to commit murder because they do not believe abortion is murder. And generals who favor Star Wars or MX missiles do not intend to stir up war because they believe these measures will increase the prospects for peace. Thus to call such people murderers or warmongers is to ignore their moral intentions. It is also to ignore strategic questions about how best to convince opponents and the larger public.

[7]The most recent abortion statistics come from the Center for Disease Control, a federal agency. In its Morbidity and Mortality Weekly Report, 6 July 1984 (the most recent statistics available), they report 1,300,760 abortions for 1981 with 38 states reporting. Actual numbers of annual abortions in America are much higher.

[8]Kenneth Kantzer, *Christianity Today,* 19 Apr. 1985, p. 223.

[9]James W. Skillen, "Justice for the Unborn" (An Association for Public Justice Position Paper, Box 56348, Washington, D.C. 20011), pp. 4-5.

[10]Akron vs. Akron Center for Reproductive Health, 51 U.S.L.W. at 4778 (1983).

[11]For an exhaustive study of the various Human Life Amendment proposals, see James Bopp, Jr., "An Examination of Proposals for a Human Life Amendment," *Restoring the Right to Life* (Provo, Utah: Brigham Young University Press, 1984), pp. 3-53.

[12]I owe this point to Juli Loesch, a founder of Prolifers for Survival.

[13]See Stephen H. Galebach, "A Human Life Statute," *Human Life Review* 7, no. 1 (Winter 1981):9-12.

[14]Harris vs. McRae, 448 U.S. 297 (1980).

[15]Belloti vs. Baird, 443 U.S. 672 (1979).

[16]Fischer vs. Commonwealth of Pennsylvania, No. 283 C. D. (1981), p. 21.

[17]Feminists for Life of America, 811 East 47th Street, Kansas City, MO 64110 (816-753-2130).

[18]See Douglas Johnson and Paige Comstock Cunningham, "ERA and Abortion: Really Separate Issues," *America,* 9 June 1984, pp. 432-37. For a dispassionate legal analysis, see Karen J. Lewis, "A Legal Analysis of the Potential Impact of the Proposed Equal Rights Amendment on the Right to an Abortion or the Funding of an Abortion," Congressional Research Service, The Library of Congress, 20 Oct. 1983.

[19]A disconcerting number of studies are being published in prestigious medical journals on the results of fetal experimentation. For details of specific experiments both in the United States and abroad, see Young, *Least of These,* pp. 101-8.

[20]Ibid., pp. 109-21. See also Melinda Delahoyde and Dennis Horan, *Infanticide* (Provo, Utah: Brigham Young University Press, 1981).

[21]Two helpful summaries of various legislative proposals are David N. O'Steen and Darla St. Martin, "Legislating Life," *Arresting Abortion,* John W. Whitehead, ed. (Westchester, Ill.: Crossway, 1985), pp. 106-16; and Lisa Andrusko, "Pro-Life Legislation in Congress, the Margin of Victory: A Winning Campaign Strategy

Handbook for Pro-Life Candidates" (an in-house document published by the National Right to Life Political Action Committee), pp. VI-1—VI-E-1. For an assessment and update of current legislation, see the legislative alerts from organizations such as the Christian Action Council, 701 West Broad Street, Suite 405, Falls Church, VA 22046; or the National Right to Life Committee, 419 7th Street, NW, Suite 402, Washington, DC 20004.

[22]A good organization to be in touch with which monitors current adoption laws and regulations is the National Committee for Adoption, Suite 512, 2025 M Street, NW, Washington, DC 20036.

Chapter 4: Both Justice and Freedom

[1]John Paul II, from an address on "Christian Unity in a Technological Age," Toronto, 14 Sept. 1984, in *Origins,* 4 Oct. 1984, p. 248.

[2]This chapter builds on chapters 3-6 of Ronald J. Sider, *Rich Christians in an Age of Hunger,* rev. ed. (Downers Grove, Ill.: InterVarsity Press, 1984). Readers interested in the relevant literature (which is vast and varied) should see the literature cited in *Rich Christians,* as well as Michael Novak, *The Spirit of Democratic Capitalism* (New York: Simon and Schuster, 1982); and S. Philip Wogaman, *The Great Economic Debate* (Philadelphia: Westminster, 1977).

[3]See the excellent encyclical on work, *Laborem Exercens* by Pope John Paul II, in Gregory Baum, *The Priority of Labor* (New York: Paulist, 1982), pp. 93-149.

[4]From the first draft of the U.S. Catholic Bishops Pastoral letter on "Catholic Social Teaching and the U.S. Economy," section 77 in *Origins,* 15 Nov. 1984, p. 349.

[5]See the fascinating development of this in the first centuries of the Christian church in Charles Avila, *Ownership: Early Christian Teaching* (Maryknoll, N.Y.: Orbis, 1984).

[6]From "Biblical Faith and Our Economic Life," adapted by the Reformed Church of America, *The Acts and Proceedings of the 178th Regular Session of the General Synod, Reformed Church of America* 64 (1984):59.

Chapter 5: On Implementing Justice

[1]Bernardin, "Seamless Garment," p. 7.

[2]Donald Granberg, "What Does It Mean to Be Pro-Life?" *Christian Century,* 12 May 1982, p. 564.

[3]See Sider, *Rich Christians.*

[4]U.S. Bureau of the Census, Current Population Reports: Consumer Income, Series P-60, no. 147, *Characteristics of the Population Below the Poverty Level: 1983* (Washington: Government Printing Office, February 1985), p. 1. See also the Dec. 1985 issue of *Seeds* which is devoted to "Hunger in America."

[5]Ibid., pp. 118-20; Robert Pear, "Study Finds Poverty among Children Is Increasing," *New York Times,* 23 May 1985 (reporting on the study of the Congressional Budget Office and the Congressional Research Service).

[6]C. Arden Miller, "Infant Mortality in the U.S.," *Scientific American* 235, no. 1 (July 1985):31-35.

[7]Massachusetts Department of Public Health, *Massachusetts Nutrition Survey* (Boston, 1983).

[8]Spencer Rich, "Report Says 20 Million Go Hungry," *Washington Post*, 27 Feb. 1985 (reporting on *Hunger in America*, a report by the Physician Task Force on Hunger).

[9]Robert Kuttner, *Equality and Efficiency* (Boston: Houghton Mifflin, 1984), pp. 46-69, 259-60; Ira C. Magaziner and Robert B. Reich, *Minding America's Business* (New York: Harcourt Brace Jovanovich, 1982), p. 25.

[10]John L. Palmer and Isabel V. Sawhill, *The Reagan Record* (Washington: Urban Institute Press, 1984), p. 352.

[11]Kuttner, *Equality and Efficiency*, pp. 259-60.

[12]Marilyn Moon and Isabel V. Sawhill, "Family Incomes: Gainers and Losers," in Palmer and Sawhill, *Reagan Record*, pp. 317-46; Christopher Jencks, "The Hidden Prosperity of the 1970s," *Public Interest*, no. 77 (Fall 1984):37, 59-60; Spencer Rich, "Income Disparities Increased in 1980-83," *Washington Post*, 8 July 1985 (reporting on Census Bureau study); Thomas J. Lueck, "Rich and Poor," *New York Times*, 2 May 1986. See also the even more disturbing report of the Congressional Joint Economic Committee released on 25 July 1986. The richest families (1/2 of 1%) held 25% of U.S. wealth in 1963 and 35% in 1983 (Ebbe and Mail, 26 July 1986, p. 1).

[13]U.S. Department of Labor, Bureau of Labor Statistics, *Monthly Labor Review* 108, no. 7 (July 1985):66.

[14]*Characteristics of the Population Below the Poverty Level: 1983*, pp. 49-50.

[15]Charles E. Lindblom, *Politics and Markets* (New York: Basic Books, 1977), p. 49.

[16]Charles Murray, *Losing Ground: American Social Policy 1950-1980* (New York: Basic Books, 1984).

[17]H. R. Rodgers, Jr., *The Cost of Human Neglect: America's Welfare Failure* (Armonk, N.Y.: W. E. Sharpe, 1982); Sar A. Levitan and Clifford M. Johnson, *Beyond the Safety Net: Reviving the Promise of Opportunity in America* (Cambridge, Mass.: Ballinger, 1984).

[18]For example, Murray, *Losing Ground*, pp. 227-28. George Gilder, *Wealth and Poverty* (New York: Bantam, 1981), pp. 139-54, is somewhat less radical.

[19]Committee on Ways and Means, U.S. House of Representatives, *Background Materials and Data on Programs within the Jurisdiction of the Committee on Ways and Means* (Committee Print, 98th Congress, 2nd Session, February 1984), pp. 299-300.

[20]Ibid.

[21]Spencer Rich, "Food-Stamp, Welfare Benefits Down," *Washington Post*, 24 Mar. 1985 (Reporting on House Ways and Means Committee Report).

[22]*Background Materials and Data on Programs*, p. 324.

[23]D. Lee Bawden and Robert L. Palmer, "Social Policy," in Palmer and Sawhill,

Reagan Record, p. 199.

[24]Martin Rein and Lee Rainwater, "Patterns of Welfare Use," *Social Services Review* 52, no. 10 (Dec. 1978):511-34. See also Maurice Emsellem and Barbara H. Linden, "Functions of Welfare: A Review of the Longitudinal Research on AFDC Households," *Clearinghouse Review* 17, no. 12 (Dec. 1983):850-59; G. J. Duncan, *Years of Poverty, Years of Plenty: The Changing Economic Fortunes of American Workers and Their Families* (Ann Arbor, Mich.: Institute for Social Research, University of Michigan, 1984); and Maurice MacDonald and Isabel V. Sawhill, "Welfare Policy and the Family," *Public Policy* 26, no. 1 (Winter 1978), pp. 113-15.

[25]Henry J. Aaron, "Six Welfare Questions Still Searching for Answers," *Brookings Review* 3, no. 10 (Fall 1984):12-17; Bawden and Palmer, "Social Policy," pp. 194-201.

[26]See Alecia Swasy, "Welfare Programs," *Wall Street Journal,* 5 Aug. 1985; and the editorial in *USA Today,* 30 Sept. 1985.

[27]See Levitan and Johnson, *Beyond the Safety Net,* pp. 61-66.

[28]Marjorie Honig, "The Impact of Welfare Payment Levels on Family Stability," in Joint Economic Committee, U.S. Congress, *Studies in Public Welfare* (Washington: Government Printing Office, 1974), pp. 37-53.

[29]Aaron, "Six Welfare Questions Still Searching for Answers," pp. 14-15.

[30]*Background Materials and Data on Programs,* pp. 299-300.

[31]June A. O'Neill, Douglas A. Wolf, Laurie J. Bassi and Michael T. Hannan, "An Analysis of Time on Welfare," Urban Institute, 1985.

[32]Rein and Rainwater, "Patterns of Welfare Use."

[33]Mary Jo Bane and David T. Ellwood, "The Dynamics of Dependence: The Routes to Self-Sufficiency" (Cambridge, Mass.: Urban Systems Research and Engineering, Inc., June 1983).

[34]A bipartisan report of the House Select Committee on Children, Youth and Families found that a number of such programs saved more money in future social costs than the programs cost. These included the Childhood Immunization Program; Women, Infant and Children (WIC) Feeding Program; prenatal health programs; preschool programs such as Head Start; compensatory education for disadvantaged children under Title I (now Chapter I) of the Elementary and Secondary Education Act; preschool education for handicapped children; and the Job Corps (Spencer Rich, "Aid to Poor Seen As Cost Effective," *Washington Post,* 15 Aug. 1985). See also Bawden and Palmer, "Social Policy," p. 201: Larry Rohter, "Study Stresses Preschool Benefits," *New York Times,* 9 Apr. 1985; Jonathan Rauch, "Women and Children's Food Program Is 'Off Limits' to Reagan Budget Cutbacks," *National Journal,* 17 Nov. 1984, pp. 2197-99.

[35]Roscoe L. Egger, Jr., "Without Real Reform, Our Tax System Could Collapse," *Washington Post,* 10 Feb. 1985.

[36]See Joseph A. Pechman, *Federal Tax Policy,* 4th ed. (Washington: Brookings

Institution, 1984), p. 5; Joseph J. Minarik, *Making Tax Choices* (Washington: Urban Institute Press, 1985), pp. 21-24, 49-51; Ronald Pasquariello, *Religious and Ethical Issues in Tax Policy* (Washington: Center for Theology and Public Policy, 1985).

[37]Joseph A. Pechman, *Who Paid the Taxes, 1966-85?* (Washington: Brookings Institution, 1985), pp. 4, 77, 80.

[38]See, for instance, Henry J. Aaron and Harvey Galper, *Assessing Tax Reform* (Washington: Brookings Institution, 1985); Joseph A Pechman, ed., *Options for Tax Reform* (Washington: Brookings Institution, 1984); Minarik, *Making Tax Choices*.

[39]Minarik, *Making Tax Choices*, pp. 90-101; Pechman, *Federal Tax Policy*, pp. 201-4; Henry J. Aaron and Harvey Galper, "A Tax on Consumption, Bequests, and Gifts and Other Strategies for Reform," in Pechman, ed., *Options for Tax Reform*, pp. 106-46.

[40]Minarik, *Making Tax Choices*, pp. 83-91; Pechman, *Federal Tax Policy*, pp. 193-201.

[41]U.S. Congress, Joint Committee on Taxation, *Federal Tax Treatment of Families Below the Poverty Line*, 9 Apr. 1984, pp. 3-9.

[42]Robert S. McIntyre and Dean E. Tipps, *Inequity and Decline* (Washington: Center on Budget and Policy Priorities, 1983), p. 13; Minarik, *Making Tax Choices*, pp. 44-46; Pechman, *Federal Tax Policy*, pp. 206-25.

[43]The personal exemption is the familiar provision which exempts $1,040 (in 1985) for the taxpayer, spouse and each dependent. From 1948 to 1970 it was set at $600; it was gradually increased in the 1970s and reached $1,000 in 1979. But were it to reflect all the inflation since 1948, it would now be worth $5,600!

The standard deduction, used by taxpayers who do not itemize their deductions (which includes nearly all poor families), was set at 10% of adjusted gross income up to a maximum deduction of $1,000 from 1944 to 1969. After gradually rising in the 1970s, it was changed in 1979 to a flat $2,300 for a single person and $3,400 for a married couple.

The earned-income tax credit was adopted in 1975 to reduce the burden of the Social Security tax on low-income workers with children and to increase work incentives. The credit originally was set at 10% of earned income (for example, wage and salary income) up to $5,000 of income and phased down to zero when income reached $10,000. In 1984, the percentage was raised to 11%, making the maximum available credit $550. If the credit reduces the income tax below zero, the taxpayer receives a payment from the government. See Minarik, *Making Tax Choices*, pp. 28, 34-36, 40-41; Pechman, *Federal Tax Policy*, pp. 75-81, 103-4, 355.

[44]Robert Kuttner, *The Economic Illusion: False Choices Between Prosperity and Social Justice* (Boston: Houghton Mifflin, 1984), pp. 223-25.

[45]Ibid., p. 198.

[46]Minarik, *Making Tax Choices*, p. 46.

⁴⁷Robert S. McIntyre and Robert Folen, *Corporate Income Taxes in the Reagan Years* (Washington: Citizens for Tax Justice, October 1984).

⁴⁸Jane Seaberry, "More Imports, Less Investment Predicted at End of Tax Trail," *Washington Post,* 18 Aug. 1986.

⁴⁹James Meade, *Efficiency, Equality and the Ownership of Property* (Cambridge: Harvard University Press, 1965), p. 39.

⁵⁰Pechman, *Federal Tax Policy,* pp. 263-64; some economists believe the tax is progressive, however.

⁵¹Ibid., pp. 245-56; Kuttner, *The Economic Illusion,* p. 205.

⁵²Pechman, *Federal Tax Policy,* p. 225; Kuttner, *The Economic Illusion,* pp. 205, 207.

⁵³Pechman, *Federal Tax Policy,* p. 225.

⁵⁴Ibid., pp. 228-30.

⁵⁵Ibid., pp. 242-43.

⁵⁶For a different view, see Gilder, *Wealth and Poverty,* esp. pp. 203-24 or John Jefferson Davis, *Your Wealth in God's World* (Phillipsburg, N.J.: Presbyterian and Reformed, 1984).

Chapter 6: The Biblical Promise

¹"One flesh" is the literal meaning of the Greek in this passage.

²See many more examples in Elizabeth Achtemeier, *The Committed Marriage* (Philadelphia: Westminster, 1976), pp. 16-17. This is probably the best available book on the theology of marriage.

³Brigette and Peter L. Berger, *The War Over the Family: Capturing the Middle Ground* (Garden City, N.Y.: Anchor Books, 1984), p. 122.

⁴Achtemeier, *Committed Marriage,* p. 44.

⁵Richard J. Foster, "God's Gift of Sexuality," *Sojourners,* July 1985, p. 16.

⁶Also, Deut 22:22-24; Lev 20:10; Jer 7:9ff.; Rom 2:22; Jas 2:11 and others.

⁷Also, Acts 15:20, 29; 21:25; 1 Cor 6:15-20; 1 Thess 4:3-4.

⁸Foster, "God's Gift of Sexuality," p. 17.

⁹Achtemeier, *Committed Marriage,* p. 162. The concept of the "unitive" function is from Achtemeier.

¹⁰Ibid.

¹¹This point is repeatedly made by Richard Lovelace in the best book on the subject, *Homosexuality and the Church: Crisis, Conflict, Compassion* (Old Tappan, N.Y.: Revell, 1978).

¹²See especially D. Sherwin Bailey, *Homosexuality and the Western Christian Tradition* (New York: Longmans, Green, 1955); John J. McNeill, *The Church and the Homosexual* (Kansas City: Sheed, Andrews and McMeel, 1976); Letha Scanzoni and Virginia R. Mollenkott, *Is the Homosexual My Neighbor?* (New York: Harper and Row, 1978).

¹³There is debate over the meaning of the Greek words translated "homosexuals," but Richard Lovelace argues convincingly for the interpretation assumed in the text, *Homosexuality and the Church,* pp. 96-98.

[14]Ibid., pp. 86-116 has an excellent critique of this special pleading.

[15]See, for instance, the studies of Neil M. Malamuth, who has shown that viewing sexual violence against women makes men more likely to commit such violence: Neil M. Malamuth and James V. P. Check, "The Effects of Mass Media Exposure on Acceptance of Violence Against Women," *Journal of Research in Personality* 15 (1981):436-46. For bibliographical reference to similar studies, see David G. Myers, *Social Psychology* (New York: McGraw Hill, 1983), p. 620; see also the discussion on pp. 361-65.

[16]See the book edited by Tom Minnery, *Pornography: A Human Tragedy* (Wheaton: Tyndale, 1986); chapters by Stephen Monsma, David Leigh and Bruce Taylor outline the legal situation. Section three provides exciting stories of victories citizens have already won.

[17]See Kenneth Kenniston, *All Our Children: The American Family Under Pressure* (New York: Harcourt, Brace and Jovanovich, 1977); and the critique in Lewis B. Smedes, *Mere Morality: What God Expects from Ordinary People* (Grand Rapids: Eerdmans, 1983), pp. 74-76.

[18]Jackie M. Smith, ed., *Women, Faith and Economic Justice* (Philadelphia: Westminster Press, 1985), p. 24.

[19]The Bergers seem to think that mothers are innately better at "mothering" than fathers. "If such an arrangement [a male as the 'mother figure'] were viable for the development of healthy infants, the vast variety of family arrangements in differing cultures would make one expect that it would have been successfully tried somewhere!" *(War Over the Family*, p. 153).

[20]*Newsweek*, 15 July 1985, pp. 42ff.

[21]Berger, *War Over the Family*, p. 162.

[22]See pp. 118-19 and n. 29 for my definition of *extreme feminism*.

[23]See Christopher J. H. Wright, *An Eye for An Eye: The Place of Old Testament Ethics Today* (Downers Grove, Ill.: InterVarsity Press, 1983), pp. 37-38, 183-85, 190-93. See also the unpublished study by Michael Schluter and Roy Clements, "Family Policy in OT Israel: Some Lessons for British Social Policy in the 1980's" (Write to 114 Barton Road, Cambridge, U.K.).

[24]Wright, *Eye for An Eye*, p. 37; Schluter and Clements "Family Policy," pp. 10, 17.

[25]Schluter and Clements, "Family Policy," pp. 10, 14.

[26]See Wright, *Eye for An Eye*, chaps. 2, 4.

[27]See ibid., pp. 37-38.

[28]Norman Gottwald, *The Tribes of Jahweh: A Sociology of the Religion of Liberated Israel 1250-1050 BC* (London: SCM Press, 1980), p. 10.

[29]See, for instance, Roxanne Dunbar in Mary Lou Thompson, ed., *Voices of the New Feminism* (Boston: Beacon, 1970); and Mary Daly's "Feminist Post Christian Introduction" to the second edition of her *The Church and the Second Sex*, 2d ed. (New York: Harper and Row, 1975).

[30]This chart is taken from Smith, ed., *Women, Faith and Economic Justice*, p. 25. The data for the chart comes from *Community and Consumer Relations*, American

Council of Life Insurance, 1850 K Street NW, Washington, DC 20006, and is used by permission.

[31]Achtemeier, *Committed Marriage,* p. 74.

[32]See C. F. D. Moule, ed., *The Significance of the Message of the Resurrection for Faith in Jesus Christ* (London: SCM Press, 1968), p. 9.

[33]See Leonard Swidler, *Biblical Affirmations of Women* (Philadelphia: Westminster, 1979), pp. 154-57.

[34]For a careful treatment of 1 Corinthians 14:34-36, see Wheaton College professor Gilbert Bilezikian, *Beyond Sex Roles: A Guide for the Study of Female Roles in the Bible* (Grand Rapids: Baker, 1985), pp. 144-53. Bilezikian argues that the call for women's silence came from Judaizing groups whom Paul rebukes. On 1 Timothy 2:11-15, see ibid., pp. 173-84, and Richard and Catherine Clark Kroeger, "May Women Teach?" *The Reformed Journal,* Oct. 1980, pp. 14-18. See also John Howard Yoder, *Politics of Jesus* (Grand Rapids: Eerdmans, 1972), pp. 163-92. For a careful, more conservative view, see George W. Knight, *The New Testament Teaching on the Role Relationship of Men and Women* (Grand Rapids: Baker, 1977).

[35]Achtemeier, *Committed Marriage,* pp. 86-87.

Chapter 7: The Family and Public Policy

[1]Armand Nicholi, "The Impact of Parental Absence on Childhood Development," *Journal of Family and Culture* 1, no. 3 (Autumn 1985):20.

[2]See two articles in a recent issue of the *Washington Monthly,* Deborah Baldwin, "The Part-Time Solution," *Washington Monthly* 16, no. 11 (Dec. 1984):25-29; Phillip Keisling, "Why Parents Think They Can't Stay Home," *Washington Monthly* 16, no. 11 (Dec. 1984):30-32.

[3]For an account of the development of that idea, see Christopher Lasch, *Haven in a Heartless World: The Family Besieged* (New York: Basic Books, 1977), pp. 97-133; and Brigitte Berger and Peter L. Berger, *War Over the Family,* pp. 32-36.

[4]See Berger and Berger, *War Over the Family,* pp. 198-99 for these two alternatives.

[5]Ibid., p. 209.

[6]Joseph Goldstein, Anna Freud and Albert J. Solnit, *Beyond the Best Interests of the Child,* rev. ed. (New York: The Free Press, 1979), p. 31.

[7]Joseph Goldstein, Anna Freud and Albert J. Solnit, *Before the Best Interests of the Child* (New York: The Free Press, 1979), p. 9 (footnotes omitted).

[8]Ibid., p. 12. See also their *Beyond the Best Interests of the Child,* pp. 49-52.

[9]Heyman and Barzelay, "The Forests and the Trees: Roe vs. Wade and its Critics," 53 *Boston University Law Review,* 765, 772-73 (1972).

[10]R. Horwitz, "John Locke and the Preservation of Liberty: A Perennial Problem of Civic Education," in *The Moral Foundations of the American Republic,* R. Horwitz, ed. (Charlottesville, Va.: University Press of Virginia, 1979), p. 131 (quoting Gordon S. Wood, *The Creation of the American Republic 1776-1787* [Chapel Hill,

N.C.: University of North Carolina Press, 1969], p. 68).

[11]Lasch, *Haven in a Heartless World,* p. 123.

[12]Ibid., p. 186.

[13]Ibid., p. 125.

[14]Heymann and Barzelay, "The Forests and the Trees," p. 773.

[15]Ibid. See also Laurence H. Tribe, *American Constitutional Law* (Mineola, N.Y.: Foundation Press, 1978), p. 1011. Tribe argues that certain decisions, such as who may bear children, "ought to be placed beyond government's reach . . . because, in government's hands, control over those choices would pose too great a danger of majority oppression or enduring subjugation."

[16]Prince vs. Massachusetts, 321 U.S. 158, 166 (1944).

[17]Loving vs. Virginia, 388 U.S. 1 (1967) invalidated a state statute which prohibited a "white person" from marrying other than a "white person." The Court stated that marriage was central "to our very existence" and concluded that the statutory restriction was unconstitutional. Giswold vs. Connecticut, 381 U.S. 479 (1965) held that the state cannot make the use of contraceptive devices or drugs by married persons a crime. The opinion of Justice Douglas stated that the marital relationship lies within a zone of privacy protected from government intrusion, a doctrine expanded in other cases involving individual privacy, most notable Roe vs. Wade, which held that a woman has a right to abortion in most circumstances. In Moore vs. City of East Cleveland, 431 U.S. 494 (1977), the Court held that an extended family, consisting of a grandmother, her son and her two grandsons (who were first cousins, not brothers), had a constitutional right to live together despite a local zoning ordinance that defined a family more narrowly.

[18]In Meyer vs. Nebraska, 262 U.S. 390 (1923), the Supreme Court struck down a state law forbidding the teaching of foreign languages to young children. The Court said that the teacher's right to teach a foreign language "and the right of the parents to engage him so to instruct their children" are protected by the Constitution (p. 400). The Court rejected the state's argument that good citizenship and patriotism would be advanced by requiring that all children have English as their mother tongue: the state "may not foster a homogeneous people with American ideals" in this manner. Although Plato may have argued for state child rearing, the Court noted, such ideas are alien to the letter and spirit of the Constitution (p. 402). In Pierce vs. Society of Sisters, 268 U.S. 510 (1925), the Court invalidated a state compulsory education statute which in effect precluded attendance at private schools. Justice McReynolds wrote that the state may not "standardize its children by forcing them to accept instruction from public school teachers only" (p. 535).

In its 1972 decision in Yoder vs. Wisconsin, 406 U.S. 205, the Court called Pierce "a charter of the rights of parents to direct the religious upbringing of their children" (p. 233). Yoder struck down a state compulsory high-school education statute as applied because it effectively would prevent Amish parents from raising their children in the Amish way of life. The Court said, "The history and culture of Western civilization reflect a strong tradition of parental concern for the nurture and upbringing of their children. This primary role of the parents in the upbringing of their children is now established beyond debate as an enduring American tradition" (p. 232).

[19]John T. Noonan, Jr., "The Family and Supreme Court," 23 *Catholic University Law Review* 264 (1973); Judith Areen, *Family Law* (Mineola, N.Y.: Foundation Press, 1978), pp. 64-212.

[20]Areen, *Family Law*, pp. 11-13; "Developments in the Law: The Constitution and the Family," 93 *Harvard Law Review* 1156, 1251, 1372 (1980) (hereinafter cited as Developments).

[21]Mary Ann Glendon, "Marriage and the State: The Withering Away of Marriage," 62 *Virginia Law Review* 663, 677-82 (1976); Jacqueline A. Priest, "Buttressing Marriage (I)," 13 *Family Law* 40 (1983), and "Buttressing Marriage (II)," 12 *Family Law* 140 (1983). Priest writes about British law, but the principles are the same.

I oppose laws which would enable a cohabiting couple to marry, without any license or legal formality, simply by registering with the state. I also oppose the continuance of "common law marriage" (where it still exists), by which a cohabiting couple who held themselves out as married could be deemed legally married after a specified period of time. But if common law marriage is abolished, the law should insure that the doctrine's salutary effects are continued, by adopting some means to protect innocent parties who believe in good faith that they are legally married but in fact are not, as when both parties are mistaken (because, for instance, the minister was not licensed to perform the ceremony), or when the innocent spouse was misled by the other (because, for instance, the other spouse was married to someone else). See Areen, *Family Law*, pp. 60-63.

[22]See Berger and Berger, *War Over the Family*, pp. 59-60; and Bruce C. Hafen, "Marriage, Kinship, and Sexual Privacy," 81 *Michigan Law Review* 464-66 (1983).

[23]No state today knowingly would issue a marriage license to a homosexual couple (Hafen, "Marriage, Kinship, and Sexual Privacy," p. 465, n. 6; Areen, *Family Law*, pp. 23-25). But arguments are made that homosexuals cannot be denied the right to marry one another, and informal marriages are entitled to the same legal protections as formal marriage (see Developments, pp. 1282-96). The City Council of West Hollywood, California, a majority of whose members are homosexual, have tentatively approved a "domestic partnership ordinance" as an alternative to a marriage license for couples, whether homosexual or not. The ordinance would grant similar treatment to such couples as to married couples in all city-run operations ("Gays May Get Marital Rights," *Washington Post*, 9 Feb. 1985). San Francisco's Board of Supervisors voted in 1982 to pay spousal benefits to unmarried partners who share "the common necessaries of life" with city employees, but the mayor vetoed the ordinance (Hafen, "Mar-

riage, Kinship, and Sexual Privacy," p. 464).

[24]Hafen, "Marriage, Kinship, and Sexual Privacy," p. 475.

[25]Ibid., p. 483 (footnote omitted).

[26]The politics of the White House Conference on Families is described in Gilbert Y. Stiner, *The Futility of Family Policy* (Washington: Brookings Institution, 1981), pp. 27-46.

[27]In 1986 the Supreme Court ruled that the Constitution does not confer a fundamental right on homosexuals to commit sodomy. The Court said that the "right to privacy" which the Court had recognized in matters of marriage, procreation, child rearing and education, contraception and abortion did not confer a right to privacy which extends to homosexual sodomy (Bowers vs. Hardwick, no. 85-140, 54 *U.S. Law Week* 4914 [30 June 1986]). This implies that the Constitution does not prevent a state from criminalizing such behavior, and certainly does not prevent a state from treating homosexual couples differently from married heterosexual couples in other areas of public policy.

[28]Areen, *Family Law,* pp. 295-310. But even in those circumstances a court could sometimes refuse to award a divorce decree. If both parties had committed one of the offenses, divorce was denied under the doctrine of recrimination. When the parties cooperated to get the divorce, it was denied on the ground of collusion. Divorce was refused on the ground of connivance when one party facilitated the adultery of the other, and on the ground of condonation if the innocent spouse had forgiven the guilty one's offense (pp. 310-23).

[29]*California Civil Code* section 4506 (West 1970).

[30]*Family Law Reporter* (Bureau of National Affairs, 1984), p. 400.

[31]See the *New York Times,* 7 Mar. 1985, reporting on a report by the National Center for Health Statistics.

[32]Robert F. Cochran, Jr., and Paul C. Vitz, "Child Protective Divorce Laws: A Response to the Effects of Parental Separation on Children," 17 *Family Law Quarterly* 327, 348 (1983).

[33]Even liberal analysts concede that the state has important reasons for regulating divorce and discouraging it, especially in families with children (Developments, pp. 1311-12).

[34]Cochran and Vitz, "Child Protective Divorce Laws," p. 343.

[35]Ibid., p. 328-43; The research of Harvard Medical School psychiatrist Armand Nicholi into the effects of parental separation from their children (by job reponsibilities, desertion, separation, divorce or death) has highlighted this link. See Armand Nicholi, speech to the Christian Legal Society Conference on Family, Law, and Public Policy, Hyannis, Mass., 22 Apr. 1983; and Armand Nicholi, "The Impact of Parental Absence on Childhood Development: An Overview of the Literature," *Journal of Family and Culture* 1, no. 3 (Autumn 1985):19-28.

[36]Cochran and Vitz, "Child Protective Divorce Laws," pp. 343-62.

[37]Custody refers to legal custody, not physical custody. Joint custody means that

the parents make decisions together about the child's life—where he resides, how he is educated and the like. The alternative is custody with one parent who makes the decisions alone, but who may be required by the court to allow the child to visit the other parent. See Areen, *Family Law*, pp. 562-67.

[38]Judy Mann, "Disastrous Divorce Results," *Washington Post*, 2 Oct. 1985.

[39]U.S. Bureau of the Census, Current Population Reports, Consumer Income, Series P-60, No. 147, *Characteristics of the Population Below the Poverty Level: 1983* (Washington: Government Printing Office, Feb. 1985), p. 2.

[40]Quoted in Mann, "Disastrous Divorce Results."

[41]Spencer Rich, "Child Support Evasion," *Washington Post*, 12 July 1985 (reporting on Census Bureau study).

[42]Margaret Engel, "New Law Helps Parents to Collect Support Pay from Scofflaw Spouses," *Washington Post*, 1 Oct. 1985.

[43]As *parens patriae*, the state has a limited power to protect or promote the interests of certain individuals, such as children or mental incompetents, who may be unable to act in their own best interests. The *parens patriae* power over children is based on the presumption that children lack the mental competence and maturity of adults (Developments, p. 1201).

[44]Berger and Berger, *War Over the Family*, p. 71.

[45]Santosky vs. Kramer, 102 S. Ct. 1388 (1982). Such a standard proof lies between the "preponderance of the evidence" (more likely than not, or better than a fifty-per-cent chance) required to prevail in most civil lawsuits, and the "beyond a reasonable doubt" standard required in criminal cases.

[46]See Bruce C. Hafen, "Children's Liberation and the New Egalitarianism: Some Reservations About Abandoning Children to Their Rights," 1976 *Brigham Young University Law Review* 605.

[47]Henry H. Foster, Jr., and Doris Jonas Freed, "A Bill of Rights for Children," 6 *Family Law Quarterly* 343 (1972); Patricia M. Wald, "Making Sense Out of the Rights of Youth," 4 *Human Rights* 13, 15 (1974).

[48]This essentially is the holding of the Supreme Court's landmark case *In re Gault*, 387 U.S. 1 (1967).

[49]The Supreme Court said that in Ginsberg vs. New York, 390 U.S. 629 (1968). This different treatment arises because of the state's interest in the upbringing of its citizens and the parents' right to control that upbringing, two interests not present in the case of adults.

[50]See, for example, Kenneth Kantzer, "Beyond 1984: An Evangelical Agenda," *Christianity Today*, 18 Jan. 1985, pp. 14-17. Non-Christians have recognized equal access as an essential element of free-speech rights which allow teen-agers to think for themselves and grow into responsible adults. See Nat Hentoff, " 'Equal Access' Let Teen-Agers Grow Up," *Washington Post*, 13 Sept. 1985.

[51]Hafen, "Children's Liberation," pp. 654-55; Berger and Berger, *War Over the Family*, p. 70.

[52]Bruce Hafen has distinguished between rights of protection and rights of

choice. The former protect children from acts of the state or others—as in the equal access and juvenile-court examples in the text, or child abuse and neglect statutes. The latter are rights of children to make decisions with binding consequences—such as having an abortion. He argues that restricting minors' choice rights is in their best interests and is itself a form-of-protection right (Hafen, "Children's Liberation," pp. 644-50).

[53]Planned Parenthood vs. Danforth, 428 U.S. 52 (1976) struck down a state statute which required parental consent. In Belotti vs. Baird, 443 U.S. 622 (1976), the Court invalidated a state law which permitted an unmarried woman under eighteen to have an abortion only with the consent of both parents or by order of a court. In Belotti, a majority of the Court indicated, however, that they would support a requirement of parental consultation for minors who cannot convince a judge that they are mature enough to make the decision on their own. Mature minors, on the other hand, could have an abortion without parental consultation. In H. L. vs. Matheson, 450 U.S. 398 (1981), the Court did approve a requirement of parental notice for an immature minor.

[54]The Supreme Court has not ruled on the question of whether a state may prohibit the distribution of contraceptives to unmarried minors without parental consent or knowledge. It has ruled against a state law which prohibited the distribution of contraceptives to all persons under sixteen, with a majority of the justices noting the perversity and ineffectiveness of punishing fornication with the risk of pregnancy. Carey vs. Population Services International, 431 U.S. 678 (1977). Lower federal courts did strike down the so-called squeal rule, a federal regulation which required that organizations receiving federal funds must notify the parents of unmarried minors that the organization has distributed contraceptives to their children.

[55]Hafen, "Children's Liberation," pp. 656-66.

[56]Allan C. Carlson, "The Family in America—1985: A Manifesto," *Journal of Family and Culture* 1, no. 1 (Spring 1985):26-27; Bill Mattox, *Tax Reform and the Family* (Washington: Family Research Council of America, July 1985).

[57]F. E. Trainer, "A Critical Analysis of Kohlberg's Contribution to the Study of Moral Thought," *Journal for the Theory of Social Behavior* 7, no. 1 (1977); William J. Bennett and Edwin J. Delattre, "Moral Education in the Schools," *The Public Interest*, no. 50 (Winter 1978), pp. 81-98.

[58]Brigitte Berger, "The Centrality of Parents in Education," *Journal of Family and Culture* 1, no. 1 (Spring 1985), pp. 39-59. This essay is reprinted in John H. Bunzel, ed., *Challenge to American Schools; The Case for Standards and Values* (New York: Oxford University Press, 1985).

[59]See the writings of Charles L. Glenn, Jr., an Episcopal priest who is also an official in the Department of Education for the Commonwealth of Massachusetts: "Why Public Schools Don't Listen," *Christianity Today*, 20 Sept. 1985, pp. 13-16; "Religion and Public Education—Can We Stop the Fighting?" *Reformed Journal* 34, no. 6 (June 1984):7-16.

[60]Samuel E. Ericsson, Kimberlee Colby and Robert Payne, *Religious Released Time Education: The Overlooked Open Door in Public Schools* (Oak Park, Ill., and Springfield, Va.: Christian Legal Society, 1982). The Supreme Court specifically has ruled that such schemes are constitutional. Zorach vs. Clauson, 343 U.S. 306 (1952). Helpful information about designing such programs is available from the Christian Legal Society at P. O. Box 1492, Springfield, VA 22151, phone (703) 941-3192, or the National Released Time Education Association at 996 Hatch Street, Cincinnati, OH 45202, phone (513) 251-4666.

[61]Glenn, "Why Public Schools Don't Listen," p. 6; Samuel Ericsson, "The Open Door for Religious Instruction in the Public Schools" (Springfield, Va.: Christian Legal Society, n.d.)

[62]Abington vs. Schempp, 374 U.S. 203 (1963).

[63]Glenn, "Why Public Schools Don't Listen," p. 15; Ericsson, "The Open Door for Religious Instruction in the Public Schools," p. 9. See also Nicholas Pediscalzi and William E. Collie, *Teaching About Religion in Public School* (Allen, Tex.: Argus, 1977). For more information write the National Council on Religion in Public Education, University of Kansas, 1300 Oread, Lawrence, KS 66045, and the Public Education Religious Studies Center, Wright State University, Dayton, OH 45435.

[64]Glenn, "Religion and Public Education," pp. 14-15.

[65]See John E. Coons and Stephen D. Sugarman, *Education by Choice: The Case for Family Control* (Berkeley: University of California Press, 1978); Berger and Berger, *War Over the Family*, pp. 209-14; Rockne McCarthy, James W. Skillen, and William A. Harper, *Disestablishment a Second Time: Genuine Pluralism for American Schools* (Grand Rapids, Mich.: Eerdmans/Christian University Press, 1982). As the authors of this last book point out, a voucher system which includes private schools will require a new reading of the First Amendment to the Constitution to allow public funds to be used in private, religiously affiliated schools.

I believe a voucher system is preferable to a tuition tax-credit plan which some have advocated as another way to enhance parental control over education. A voucher plan would involve all parents, not just those who can afford to send their children to private school even with a partial reimbursement by the government. Moreover, tax credits are available only to those who pay taxes, which excludes (or at least it ought to if the tax system is fair) low-income families. A voucher plan would in particular help poor urban families who today have little choice but to attend poorly financed, heavily segregated urban public schools. See note 68.

[66]Denis P. Doyle and Chester E. Finn, Jr., "American Schools and the Future of Local Control," *Public Interest*, no. 77 (Fall 1984):77-95.

[67]Charles L. Glenn, Jr., "Learning from Dutch Education," *Reformed Journal* 34, no. 9 (Sept. 1984):14-17.

[68]Orlan Love, "Freedom of Choice for Inner-City Parents," *Catholic League News-*

letter, Sept. 1980 (Catholic League for Religious and Civl Rights, 1100 West Wells Street, Milwaukee, WI 53233).

[69]Both Berger and Berger, *War Over the Family,* p. 209, and Schluter and Clements "Family Policy in Old Testament Israel," p. 35 (see chapter six) make similar recommendations.

[70]See the interesting article reviewing Catholic efforts in Allen C. Carlson, "Toward a Profamily Economics," *New Oxford Review,* Nov. 1982, pp. 18-24.

[71]National Conference of Catholic Bishops, "Catholic Social Teaching and the US Economy" (first draft), para. 164 (reprinted in *Origins* 14, no. 22-23 [15 Nov. 1984], p. 359).

[72]Carlson, "The Family in America—1985: A Manifesto," p. 27.

[73]Under a progressive tax structure, tax deductions are worth more to wealthy families than they are to poor families, but tax credits benefit all taxpayers equally. For example, a taxpayer in the fifty-per-cent bracket saves fifty cents for each one dollar deducted, but a taxpayer in the eleven-per-cent bracket saves only eleven cents. A tax credit is subtracted from the amount of taxes due and is the same for everyone who pays at least that much in taxes.

[74]George Gilder, *Wealth and Poverty,* pp. 152-53; Robert Kuttner, *The Economic Illusion: False Choices Between Prosperity and Social Justice* (Boston: Houghton Mifflin, 1984), pp. 239, 243-46.

[75]Sheila B. Kammerman and Alfred J. Kahn, "The Day Care Debate: A Wider View," *Public Interest,* no. 54 (Winter 1979):90-93.

[76]Berger and Berger, *War Over the Family,* p. 205.

[77]Robert Pear, "Court Cases Reveal New Inequalities in Women's Pay," *New York Times,* 21 Aug. 1985.

[78]*The State of the Family 1984-85* (New York: Family Service America, 1984), p. 69.

[79]Office of General Counsel, United States Catholic Conference, *The Equal Rights Amendment: A Legal Assessment* (Washington: U.S. Catholic Conference, Nov. 1984), pp. 17-18. There is no federal constitutional right to public funding for abortion (Harris vs. McRae, 448 U.S. 297 [1980]). The concern is that the ERA may create one, because it would require a comprehensive medical program like Medicaid to treat men and women equally, and exclusion of abortion might be considered unequal treatment. The Court has ruled in the past, however, that exclusion of pregnancy from a state disability compensation program was not sex discrimination under current federal law (Geduldig vs. Aiello, 417 U.S. 484 [1974]). But with the added weight of the ERA, some believe that the result would change. A Pennsylvania state judge ruled that his state's ERA did create a right to public funding of abortion. But his decision was reversed on appeal by a higher state court. Nonetheless, some lawyers believe that federal courts would adopt the reasoning of the lower court judge (See Jim McManus and Steve Askin, "Court Flips Ruling That ERA Permits Abortion," *National Catholic Reporter,* 5 Oct. 1984, p. 6).

[80]Office of General Counsel, United States Catholic Conference, *The Equal Rights*

Amendment: A Legal Assessment, pp. 16-25.

Chapter 8: Christian Faith and the Nuclear Arms Race
[1]*Challenge of Peace,* sec. 15.
[2]"Statement of the Holy See to the United Nations" (1976), in *The Church and the Arms Race* (New York: Pax Christi, 1976), pp. 23-24.
[3]"What Shall We Do About the Nuclear Problem?" *Christianity Today,* 21 Jan. 1983, p. 10.
[4]See for instance, Robert G. Clouse, ed., *War: Four Christian Views* (Downers Grove, Ill.: InterVarsity Press, 1981). For the case against Christian participation in war, see the many books of John Howard Yoder, especially *Politics of Jesus* (Grand Rapids: Eerdmans, 1972); and Ronald J. Sider, *Christ and Violence* (Scottsdale, Pa.: Herald Press, 1979); Ronald J. Sider and Richard K. Taylor, *Nuclear Holocaust and Christian Hope* (Downers Grove, Ill.: InterVarsity Press, 1982), chaps. 5-8; and Stanley Hauerwas, especially *The Peaceable Kingdom* (Notre Dame, Ind.: University of Notre Dame Press, 1983); and his *Against the Nations: War and Survival in a Liberal Society* (New York: Seabury, 1985).
[5]See John Piper, *Love Your Enemies* (Cambridge, Eng.: Cambridge University Press, 1979), pp. 21-48.
[6]The best book on the history of this issue is still Roland H. Bainton, *Christian Attitudes toward War and Peace* (New York: Abingdon, 1960). See also, Sider and Taylor, *Nuclear Holocaust,* pp. 89-91.
[7]For documentation on these and the following statistics, see Sider and Taylor, *Nuclear Holocaust,* chap. 2.
[8]Quoted in *The Defense Monitor,* Feb. 1979, p. 6.
[9]U.S. Arms Control and Disarmament Agency, "Worldwide Effects of Nuclear War . . . Some Perspectives," report no. 81 (Washington: U.S. Government Printing Office, 1975), p. 5.
[10]Ibid.
[11]Arthur I. Waskow, *The Limits of Defense* (Garden City, N.Y.: Doubleday, 1962), p. 41.
[12]Robert A. Gessert and Bryan Hehir, *The New Nuclear Debate* (New York: Council on Religious and International Affairs, 1976), p. 49.
[13]Kenneth Kantzer, "What Shall We Do About the Nuclear Problem," *Christianity Today,* 21 Jan. 1983, p. 9. For John Stott, see *Christianity Today,* 8 Feb. 1980, p. 45.
[14]*Challenge of Peace,* p. 48, sect. 179.
[15]Ibid., sect. 180 and n. 82.
[16]Ibid., p. 49, sect. 180.
[17]Ken Kantzer thinks 100 million deaths might be justified ("What Shall We Do?" p. 10).
[18]Robert McNamara, Einstein Peace Prize address (italics added).
[19]Senators Gary Hart and Barry Goldwater, *Recent False Alerts from the Nation's*

Missile Attack Warning System (Washington: Government Printing Office, 1980), pp. 12-13.

[20]Lloyd J. Dumas, "Human Falliblity and Weapons," *Bulletin of the Atomic Scientists* 36 (Nov. 1980):16.

[21]Quoted in Robert W. Gardiner, *The Cool Arm of Destruction* (Philadelphia: Westminster, 1974), p. 63.

Chapter 9: Building Peace in the Nuclear Age

[1]John Paul II, Coventry, 1982.

[2]*Challenge of Peace*, p. 11.

[3]McGeorge Bundy, "Strategic Deterrence Thirty Years Later: What Has Changed?" *The Future of Strategic Deterrence*, Part 1, Adelphi Papers, no. 160 (London, 1980), p. 6 (Bundy is partly summarizing and partly quoting Brodie.)

[4]I do not, however, hide the fact that I do not finally accept the just war tradition, although I respect those who do. In Sider and Taylor, *Nuclear Holocaust*, I develop a pacifist or nonviolent approach grounded in the teachings of Jesus. And I show how the defense of freedom, justice, democracy and national integrity is possible in a nonviolent way. Richard Taylor and I are currently working on another book to develop this argument further: *Can We Defend Democracy without (Nuclear) Weapons?*

[5]*Challenge of Peace*, p. 68.

[6]Quoted in Commission on Peace, Episcopal Diocese of Washington, D.C., *The Nuclear Dilemma: A Search for Christian Understanding* (Washington, 1983), p. 37.

[7]Ibid., p. 8.

[8]Quoted in ibid.

[9]Michael Mandelbaum, *The Nuclear Question* (Cambridge, Eng.: Cambridge Univ. Press, 1979), p. 47.

[10]Laurence Martin, "The Determinants of Change: Deterrence and Technology," *The Future of Strategic Deterrence*, Part 2, Adelphi Papers, no. 161 (London 1980), p. 10.

[11]Quoted in Eugene J. Carroll, "Nuclear Weapons and Deterrence," *The Nuclear Crisis Reader* (New York: Random House, 1984), p. 7.

[12]Ibid., p. 8.

[13]Ibid.

[14]Quoted in ibid.

[15]For further treatment, see ibid; K. D. Johnson, "The Morality of Nuclear Deterrence," *The Nuclear Crisis Reader* (New York: Random House, 1984). Robert S. McNamara and Hans A. Bethe, *Reducing the Risk of Nuclear War: Geneva Can Be a Giant Step Toward a More Secure Twenty-first Century* (Washington: CSI Studies, 1985).

[16]Thomas C. Schelling, "What Went Wrong with Arms Control?" *Foreign Affairs*, Winter 1985/86, p. 219.

[17]The Harvard Nuclear Study Group, "The Realities of Arms Control," *Atlantic*

Monthly, June 1983, p. 49.

[18]McGeorge Bundy, George F. Kennan, Robert S. McNamara, Gerard Smith, "Nuclear Weapons and the Atlantic Alliance," *No First-Use* (London: Taylor & Francis, 1984), p. 40.

[19]"The Realities of Arms Control," p. 46.

[20]Quoted in Sidney Drell, Philip Farley, David Holloway, "The Reagan Strategic Defense Initiative," excerpted in *Arms Control Today,* July/Aug. 1984, p. 10.

[21]Quoted in McNamara and Bethe, *Reducing the Risk of Nuclear War,* p. 5.

[22]Drell, Farley, Holloway, "The Reagan Strategic Defense Initiative," p. 10.

[23]McGeorge Bundy, "The Relation Between Star Wars and Arms Control," *Arms Control Today,* Apr. 1985, p. 3.

[24]Ibid.

[25]Patrick Leahy, "The Future of the Freeze," *Arms Control Today,* Oct. 1983, p. 2.

[26]Center for Defense Information, "Simultaneous Test Ban: A Primer on Nuclear Explosions," *The Defense Monitor,* 1985, p. 9.

[27]"The Realities of Arms Control," p. 46.

[28]"Simultaneous Test Ban," p. 1.

[29]Ibid., p. 3.

[30]Ibid., p. 10.

[31]"Nuclear Disarmament by the Year 2000: Statement by Mikhail Gorbachev, General Secretary of the CPSU Central Committee," reprinted in the *New York Times,* 5 Feb. 1986.

[32]James W. Skillen, Theodore R. Malloch, Jr., *Just Defense and Nuclear Weapons* (Washington: Association for Public Justice, 1983), p. 31.

[33]*The Nuclear Dilemma,* p. 23. This, however, is not my own position. I oppose "unilateral disarmament" if that means deciding to do nothing to defend freedom, democracy and justice. But I believe Christians must follow Jesus' nonviolent way no matter what others do. For my careful development of this approach, see Sider and Taylor, *Nuclear Holocaust* (and n. 4 earlier).

[34]*The Nuclear Dilemma,* p. 65.

[35]Ibid.

[36]Bundy, "Strategic Deterrence Thirty Years Later," p. 8.

Chapter 10: Toward a Comprehensive Vision

[1]Bernard F. Law, "The Consistent Prolife Ethic," *New Oxford Review,* Jan.-Feb. 1985, p. 9.

[2]*Newsweek,* 8 Mar. 1982, p. 89.

[3]William Pollin, "The Role of the Addictive Process as a Key Step in Causation of All Tobacco-Related Diseases," *Journal of the American Medical Association* (JAMA) 252 (23-30 Nov. 1984):2874.

[4]Peter Taylor, *The Smoke Ring: Tobacco, Money and Multinational Politics* (New York: Pantheon, 1984), p. xvii.

[5]Michael Crosby, "Selling Cigarettes to the Third World," *Christianity and Crisis,*

30 May 1983, p. 212.

[6]Pollin, "Role of the Addictive Process," p. 2874.

[7]Ibid. See also William Pollin's and R. T. Ravenholt's longer article in the same issue of JAMA: "Tobacco Addiction and Tobacco Mortality" (pp. 2849-54).

[8]David Owen, "The Cigarette Companies: How They Get Away with Murder, Part II," *Washington Monthly*, Mar. 1985, p. 50. See also Ken Cummins, "The Cigarette Makers: How They Get Away with Murder," *Washington Monthly*, Apr. 1984, pp. 14-24.

[9]Lindsey Gruson, "Employers Get Tough on Smoking at Work," *New York Times*, 14 Mar. 1985.

[10]Owen, "The Cigarette Companies," p. 50.

[11]Quoted in Crosby, "Selling Cigarettes to the Third World," p. 212.

[12]See the work of Owen, "The Cigarette Companies"; Cummins, "The Cigarette Makers"; and Taylor, *The Smoke Ring*.

[13]*Christianity Today*, 19 Apr. 1985, p. 44. See further, Taylor, *The Smoke Ring*; and Raymond Downing, "The Politics of Smoking," *Other Side*, Feb. 1982, pp. 15-18.

[14]Owen, "The Cigarette Companies," p. 51.

[15]Michael Jacobson, George Hacker and Robert Atkins, *The Booze Merchants: The Inebriating of America* (Washington: Center for Science in the Public Interest, 1983), p. 2.

[16]Ibid., p. 5.

[17]See the Materials on Alcohol Awareness of the Southern Baptist Churches, Christian Life Commission (460 James Robertson Parkway, Nashville, TN 37219), and their publication, *Light*, July-Aug. 1983, p. 6.

[18]Hatfield Backgrounder, July 1983, p. 1 (write Senator Mark Hatfield, Washington, DC 20510).

[19]Jacobson, Hacker and Atkins, *Booze Merchants*, p. 3.

[20]Ibid., chaps. 3-6.

[21]George Hacker, "The Inebriating of America," *Multinational Monitor*, Nov. 1983, p. 16. See also pp. 9-16 of the issue for an exposé of how the World Health Organization was pressured into dropping plans to publish a major study on the world liquor business.

[22]Write to Project SMART, P.O. Box 19125, Washington, DC 20036.

[23]See Ebenezer Sunder Raj, "The Origins of the Caste System," *Transformation*, Apr.-June 1985, p. 10. See, too, the other articles on caste in this issue.

[24]"Racial Issues Called Factor in Democratic Defections," *Philadelphia Inquirer*, 6 May 1985.

[25]See p. 120.

[26]Bureau of the Census, Statistical Abstract of the United States, (Washington: Government Printing Office, December, 1985), p. 451 (1983 data).

[27]Robert Greenstein and Laura Weiss, "Worse Under Reagan," *New York Times*. For a good discussion, see Carl F. Ellis, Jr., *Beyond Liberation* (Downers Grove, Ill.: InterVarsity Press, 1983).

[28]Wesley Granberg-Michaelson, *A Worldly Spirituality: The Call to Redeem Life on Earth* (New York: Harper, 1984), p. 8. Another good book on ecological concerns is Wilkinson, et al., *Earth Keeping*.

[29]Michaelson, *Worldly Spirituality*, p. 8.

[30]Ibid., p. 14.

[31]Ibid., pp. 15-16.

[32]For a good discussion of soft energy possibilities, see Amory B. Lovins, *Soft Energy Paths: Toward a Durable Peace* (New York: Harper, 1977).

[33]Gerald V. Barney, study director, *The Global 2000 Report to the President: Entering the Twenty-first Century*, 3 vols. (Washington: Government Printing Office, 1980) 2:364.

[34]Ibid., 2:367.

[35]See the important new book by Lutheran bishop Lowell O. Erdahl, *Pro-Life/ Pro-Peace: Life Affirming Alternatives to Abortion, War, Mercy Killing and the Death Penalty* (Minneapolis: Augsburg, 1986).

Chapter 11: A Historic Opportunity

[1]John Pollock has written one of the best biographies: *Wilberforce* (Herts, Eng.: Lion, 1977).

[2]For Finney, see Donald W. Dayton, *Discovering an Evangelical Heritage* (New York: Harper, 1976), see esp. pp. 15-24.

[3]Andrew Murray, *With Christ in the School of Prayer* (Old Tappan, N.J.: Revell, 1953), pp. 102-3.

[4]See further Ronald J. Sider, "A Plea for More Radical Conservatives and More Conserving Radicals," *Transformation* 4, no. 1 (Jan.-Mar. 1987):11-16.

Bibliography

The number of books on each of the topics dealt with in this volume is huge. Therefore, I make no attempt in this bibliography to be complete. Rather I try to point the reader to a few of the most significant books in each of the major areas discussed in the book. (Books that agree and disagree with the argument developed in this book are included.)

Abortion

Davis, John Jefferson. *Abortion and the Christian*. Phillipsburg, N.J.: Presbyterian and Reformed Press, 1984.

Fletcher, Joseph. *Morals and Medicine*. Princeton: Princeton University Press, 1954.

Gorman, Michael J. *Abortion and the Early Church*. Downers Grove, Ill.: InterVarsity Press, 1982.

Harrison, Beverly Wildung. *Our Right to Choose: Toward a New Ethic of Abortion*. Boston: Beacon Press, 1983.

Jones, D. Gareth. *Brave New People*. Grand Rapids: Eerdmans, 1985.

Luker, Kristin. *Abortion and the Politics of Motherhood*. Berkeley: University of California Press, 1984.

Montgomery, John Warwick. *Slaughter of the Innocents*. Westchester, Ill.: Crossway, 1981.

Noonan, John T. *The Morality of Abortion: Legal and Historical Perspectives*. Cambridge, Mass.: Harvard University Press, 1970.

O'Donovan, Oliver. *The Christian and the Unborn Child.* 2d ed. Bramcote Notts, Eng.: Grove Books, 1975.

Report of the Committee to Study the Matter of Abortion. *Minutes of the Thirty-Eighth General Assembly.* The Orthodox Presbyterian Church, 7401 Old York Road, Philadelphia, PA 19126.

Young, Curt. *The Least of These.* Chicago: Moody Press, 1983.

Economics

Avila, Charles. *Ownership: Early Christian Teaching.* Maryknoll, N.Y.: Orbis, 1984.

Baum, Gregory. *The Priority of Labor.* New York: Paulist, 1982.

Benne, Robert. *The Ethic of Democratic Capitalism.* Philadelphia: Fortress, 1981.

Davis, John Jefferson. *Your Wealth in God's World.* Phillipsburg, N.J.: Presbyterian and Reformed, 1984.

Duncan, G. J. *Years of Poverty, Years of Plenty: The Changing Economic Fortunes of American Workers and Their Families.* Ann Arbor: Institute for Social Research, University of Michigan, 1984.

Goudzwaard, Bob. *Capitalism and Progress.* Grand Rapids: Eerdmans, 1979.

Grant, George. *Bringing in the Sheaves: Transforming Poverty into Productivity.* Atlanta: American Vision Press, 1985.

Griffiths, Brian. *Morality and the Market Place.* London: Hodder and Stoughton, 1982.

Klay, Robin Kendrick. *Counting the Cost: The Economics of Christian Stewardship.* Grand Rapids: Eerdmans, 1986.

Levitan, Sar A., and Johnson, Clifford M. *Beyond the Safety Net: Reviving the Promise of Opportunity in America.* Cambridge, Mass.: Ballinger, 1984.

Murray, Charles. *Losing Ground: American Social Policy 1950-1980.* New York: Basic Books, 1984.

Nelson, Jack A. *Hunger for Justice: The Politics of Food and Faith.* Maryknoll, N.Y.: Orbis, 1981.

Novak, Michael. *The Spirit of Democratic Capitalism.* New York: Simon and Schuster, 1982.

Palmer, John L., and Sawhill, Isabel V. *The Reagan Record.* Washington: Urban Institute Press, 1984.

Pasquariello, Ronald. *Religious and Ethical Issues in Tax Policy.* Washington: Center for Theology and Public Policy, 1985.

Pechman, Joseph A. *Federal Tax Policy.* 4th ed. Washington: Brookings Institution, 1984.

——————— . *Who Paid the Taxes, 1966-85?* Washington: Brookings Institution, 1985.

Pemberton, Prentiss L., and Finn, Daniel Rush. *Toward a Christian Economic Ethic.* Minneapolis: Winston Press, 1985.

Sider, Ronald J., ed. *Cry Justice.* New York: Paulist; and Downers Grove, Ill.:

InterVarsity Press, 1980.

_____ . *Rich Christians in an Age of Hunger.* Rev ed. Downers Grove, Ill.: InterVarsity Press, 1984.

Wogaman, J. Philip. *Economics and Ethics: A Christian Inquiry.* Philadelphia: Fortress, 1986.

_____ . *The Great Economic Debate.* Philadelphia: Westminster, 1977.

Family

Achtemeier, Elizabeth. *The Committed Marriage.* Philadelphia: Westminster, 1976.

Anderson, Ray S., and Guernsey, Dennis B. *On Being Family: A Social Theology of the Family.* Grand Rapids: Eerdmans, 1985.

Berger, Brigette and Peter L. *The War Over the Family: Capturing the Middle Ground.* Garden City, N.Y.: Anchor Books, 1984.

Drescher, John M. and Betty. *If We Were Starting Our Marriage Again.* Nashville: Abingdon, 1985.

Foster, Richard J. *Money, Sex, and Power.* New York: Harper & Row, 1985.

Lovelace, Richard. *Homosexuality and the Church: Crisis, Conflict, Compassion.* Old Tappan, N.J.: Revell, 1978.

Minnery, Tom, ed. *Pornography: A Human Tragedy. Compelling New Evidence on How It Hurts People.* Wheaton: Tyndale, 1986.

Olthuis, James H. *I Pledge You My Troth: A Christian View of Marriage, Family, Friendship.* San Francisco: Harper & Row, 1975.

Schmitt, Abraham and Dorothy. *Renewing Family Life.* Scottdale, Pa.: Herald Press, 1985.

Smith, Jackie, ed. *Women, Faith and Economic Justice.* Philadelphia: Westminster Press, 1985.

Nuclear Arms Race

Augsburger, Myron S., and Dean C. Curry. *Nuclear Arms: Two Views on World Peace.* Waco, Tex.: Word, 1987.

Aukerman, Dale. *Darkening Valley: A Biblical Perspective on Nuclear War.* New York: Seabury, 1981.

The Baptist Peacemaker. Deer Park Baptist Church, 1733 Bardstown Road, Louisville, KY 40205.

Beachy, Duane. *Faith in a Nuclear Age: A Christian Response to War.* Scottdale, Pa.: Herald Press, 1983.

Beres, Louis Rene. *Apocalypse: Nuclear Catastrophe in World Politics.* Chicago: University of Chicago Press, 1982.

Caldicott, Helen. *Nuclear Madness: What You Can Do.* Brookline, Mass.: Autumn Press, 1978.

Commission on Peace, Episcopal Diocese of Washington, D.C. *The Nuclear Dilemma: A Search for Christian Understanding.* Washington: Episcopal Diocese of Washington, 1983.

Davidson, Donald L. *Nuclear Weapons and the American Churches: Ethical Positions on Modern Warfare*. Boulder, Colo.: Westview Press, 1983.

The Defense Monitor. Center for Defense Information, 600 Maryland Avenue SW, Washington, DC 20024.

Disarmament Times. Room 7B, 777 United Nations Plaza, New York, NY 10017.

Dyson, Freeman J. *Weapons and Hope*. New York: Harper & Row, 1984.

The Effects of Nuclear War. Washington: U.S. Arms Control and Disarmament Agency, 1979.

Gessert, Robert A., and Hehir, J. Bryan. *The New Nuclear Debate*. New York: Council on Religion and International Affairs, 1976.

Geyer, Alan. *The Idea of Disarmament: Rethinking the Unthinkable*. Elgin, Ill.: Brethren Press, 1982.

Gremillion, Joseph, ed. *The Gospel of Peace and Justice: Catholic Social Teaching since Pope John*. Maryknoll, N.Y.: Orbis, 1976.

Hauerwas, Stanley. *The Peaceable Kingdom*. Notre Dame, Ind.: Notre Dame University Press, 1983.

————— . *Against the Nations: War and Survival in a Liberal Society*. New York: Seabury, 1985.

Kownacki, Mary Lou, ed. *A Race to Nowhere: An Arms Race Primer for Catholics*. Chicago: Pax Christi, 1980.

Kraybill, Donald. *Facing Nuclear War: A Plea for Christian Witness*. Scottdale, Pa.: Herald Press, 1982.

A Matter of Faith: A Study Guide for Churches on the Nuclear Arms Race. Washington: Sojourners Peace Ministry, 1981.

National Conference of Catholic Bishops. *The Challenge of Peace: God's Promise and Our Response*. Boston: St. Paul Editions, 1983.

Physicians for Social Responsibility. *The Final Epidemic: The Medical Consequences of Nuclear Weapons and Nuclear War*. Chicago: Educational Foundation for Nuclear Science, 1981.

Prins, Gwyn, ed. *The Nuclear Crisis Reader*. New York: Random House, 1984.

Schell, Jonathan. *The Fate of the Earth*. New York: Knopf, 1982.

Sider, Ronald J., and Taylor, Richard K. *Nuclear Holocaust and Christian Hope*. Downers Grove, Ill.: InterVarsity Press, 1982.

Sivard, Ruth L. *World Military and Social Expenditures*. Leesburg, Va.: WMSE Publications, 1981.

Wallis, Jim, ed. *Waging Peace: A Handbook in the Struggle to Abolish Nuclear Weapons*. San Francisco: Harper & Row, 1982.

Yoder, John Howard. *The Politics of Jesus*. Grand Rapids: Eerdmans, 1972.

Racism

Boesak, Allan Aubrey. *Walking on Thorns: The Call to Christian Obedience*. Grand Rapids: Eerdmans, 1984.

Bowser, Benjamin, and Hunt, Raymond G., eds. *Impacts of Racism on White Amer-*

icans. Beverly Hills, Calif.: Sage Publications, 1981.

Dunbar, Leslie W., ed. *Minority Report: What Has Happened to Blacks, Hispanics, American Indians, and other Minorities in the Eighties.* New York: Pantheon Books, 1984.

Ellis, Carl F., Jr. *Beyond Liberation.* Downers Grove, Ill.: InterVarsity Press, 1983.

Haselden, Kyle. *The Racial Problem in Christian Perspective.* New York: Harper Torchbooks, 1964.

King, Charles H. *Fire in My Bones.* Grand Rapids: Eerdmans, 1983.

Roberts, James Deotis. *Black Theology Today: Liberation and Contextualization.* New York: Edwin Mellen, 1983.

Salley, Columbus, and Behm, Robert. *What Color Is Your God?* Downers Grove, Ill.: InterVarsity Press, 1981.

Tutu, Desmond M. *Hope and Suffering.* Grand Rapids: Eerdmans, 1984.

Other Pro-Life Issues

Bernardin, Joseph. *The Seamless Garment.* Kansas City: National Catholic Reporter, 1984.

Erdahl, Lowell O. *Pro-Life/Pro-Peace: Life Affirming Alternatives to Abortion, War, Mercy Killing and the Death Penalty.* Minneapolis: Augsburg, 1986.

Granberg-Michaelson, Wesley, ed. *Tending the Garden: Essays on the Gospel and the Earth.* Grand Rapids, Mich.: Eerdmans, 1987.

————. *A Worldly Spirituality: The Call to Redeem Life on Earth.* New York: Harper, 1984.

Jacobson, Michael; Hacker, George; and Atkins, Robert. *The Booze Merchants: The Inebriating of America.* Washington: Center for Science in the Public Interest, 1983.

Lovins, Amory B. *Soft Energy Paths: Toward a Durable Peace.* New York: Harper, 1977.

Taylor, Paul. *The Smoke Ring: Tobacco, Money and Multinational Politics.* New York: Pantheon, 1984.

Wilkinson, Loren, ed. *Earth Keeping: Christian Stewardship of Natural Resources.* Grand Rapids: Eerdmans, 1980.

Index

Evangelicals for Social Action (ESA) and JustLife can help readers implement the concerns of this book. ESA is a national organization of committed Christians working to witness to the lordship of Jesus Christ in public life. Rejecting ideologies of left and right, ESA starts with biblical principles in an attempt to develop a thoroughly Christ-centered approach to a wide range of issues—the family, the nuclear arms race, abortion, hunger and economic justice. With a national membership and local chapters around the country, ESA helps individuals solve large, complex problems by enabling them to link arms with others who share a biblical approach.

For more information on ESA, write me at Evangelicals for Social Action, 5107 Newhall Street, Philadelphia, PA 19144 or call (215) 438-1670.

JustLife is a political action committee composed of committed Christians taking a consistent pro-life stand into electoral politics. JustLife supports candidates who work for economic justice and oppose abortion and the nuclear arms race.

For more information on JustLife, write me at JustLife, 5107 Newhall Street, Philadelphia, PA 19144, or call (215) 438-3990.

Ronald J. Sider
Executive Director of Evangelicals for Social Action and
JustLife